Here's What People Are Saying About *Chocolate for a Woman's Soul:*

"I couldn't put it down.... Men love chocolate too.... Do yourself the favor of reading this book!"

—Jack Canfield,
coauthor of *Chicken Soup for the Soul*

"Every time the heart beats, it makes an echo in the greater body. We are the greater body. This book is that clear, honest healing echo."

—Ondrea and Stephen Levine,
authors of *Embracing the Beloved*

"Just as it is impossible to eat only one piece of mouthwatering chocolate, I dare you to read only one of these heartwarming stories! Each has a special flavor and will awaken memories of your soul's deepest longing. This book is the perfect gift to send a hug and lift the spirit of a friend or loved one."

—Ann McGee-Cooper, author of
You Don't Have to Go Home from Work Exhausted!

"It is so nice to have a book with inspiring messages that can be read and absorbed in moments instead of months. Thank you for adding some soul to my life."

—C.H., Roseville, California

"After reading *Chocolate for a Woman's Soul*, I can't wait for book two!"

—D.E., Honolulu

"I was inspired by your book! It made me think of all the wonderful people and experiences that have been a part of my life."

—L.J., Evanston, Illinois

"*Chocolate for a Woman's Soul* is positive and inspiring and left me with a message. I haven't stopped thinking or talking about it."

—L.J., Irving, Texas

"I've gotten into the habit now of reading one story a day to a few coworkers. We all enjoy the stories and each have our favorite!"

—L.L.P., Lyndhurst, New Jersey

"When I need a boost of endorphins, I reach for that chocolate bar. Now when I need a boost of spirit, perspective, and endorphins, I will reach for your book."

—N.Y., Honolulu

"I wanted you to know how much I appreciate your book, *Chocolate for a Woman's Soul*. It touched my heart, my brain, and my giggle box!"

—S.D., Knoxville, Tennessee

"The book was such a wonderful gift. . . . I read it and finished it and passed it to my momma. She loves it too!"

—S.K., Portland, Oregon

"Thank you for the work you have put together in *Chocolate for a Woman's Soul*."

—S.A.R., New Orleans

ALSO BY KAY ALLENBAUGH

Chocolate for a Woman's Soul

77 Stories of Love,

Kindness, and Compassion

to Nourish Your Soul

and Sweeten Your Dreams

A FIRESIDE BOOK
Published by Simon & Schuster

Chocolate for a Woman's Heart

KAY ALLENBAUGH

FIRESIDE
Rockefeller Center
1230 Avenue of the Americas
New York, NY 10020

Copyright © 1998 by Kay Allenbaugh
All rights reserved,
including the right of reproduction
in whole or in part in any form.

FIRESIDE and colophon are registered trademarks
of Simon & Schuster Inc.

Designed by Bonni Leon

Manufactured in the United States of America

1 3 5 7 9 10 8 6 4 2

Library of Congress Cataloging-in-Publication Data is available.

ISBN 0-684-84896-1

With deep love, affection,

and heart connection,

I dedicate this book

to my daddy—

the smartest,

best-humored

man I know.

CONTENTS

Introduction   17

I
DIVINE INTERVENTION

Back-Seat Driver   *Anamae Elledge*   21

A Dream Come True   *Ursula Bacon*   23

Small Miracles   *Jill and Candis Fancher*   26

A Wise Man, a Mentor, or an Angel?   *Donna Hartley*   28

Turning Point   *Rev. Deborah Olive*   32

Divine Assistance   *Rev. Mary Omwake*   34

Earth Angel   *Ann Albers*   36

Our Teachers Come in Many Forms   *Kay Allenbaugh*   39

II
GROWTH SPURTS

Angel of the Lord   *Arline Crawford Burton*   45

Just a Hair More Love   *O. C. O'Connell*   47

Soulmating   *Catherine Lanigan*   49

Moving the Moon   *Sarah Jordan*   52

Healing with Love   *Rev. Mary Manin Morrissey*   54

The Miracle of Self-Love   *Jill Goodwin*   57

III
FEEDING A WOMAN'S HEART

Snapshots of the Heart   *Linda Dunivin*   61

The Pajama Connection   *Ellen Urbani Hiltebrand*   64

Pairs and Spares   *Liz Curtis Higgs*   68

The Lucky Photo   *Lorri Vaughter Allen*   71

Mercy Street   *Holly Fitzhardinge*   73

Love Is Not for the Faint of Heart   *Chassidy A. F. Persons*   77

Marriage Encounter   *Christine D. Marek*   80

IV
MAXIMUM EXPOSURE

Soap Box Derby   *Marci Madsen Fuller*   85

The Miracle Bus   *Jill Lynne*   88

The Power of Love   *Michelle Cohen*   90

The Virtues of Mr. Wrong!   *Jennifer Brown Banks*   94

Ginny's Excellent Adventure   *Bailey Allard*   96

My Trucker   *Constance Conace*   99

V PATHFINDERS

Pray to God and Read the Paper   *Susan LaMaire*   105

Flight of Destiny   *Robin Ryan*   107

Fern Cave   *Sharon Kinder*   110

Letter to Tim   *T. J. Banks*   113

And Baby Makes Three   *Donna Hartley*   117

It's About Time   *Nancy Kiernan*   119

VI FREE AT LAST

A Walk on the Wild Side   *Judith Morton Fraser*   125

The Warm Fuzzy Hostile Group   *Jody Stevenson*   129

Create Your Own Heaven Today   *Christine Harvey*   132

You Are My Brother   *Kathi J. Kemper*   134

The Journey Home   *Marie Hegeman*   136

Me, Myself, and I   *Stephanie Lauridsen*   140

Modeling for Life   *Joeann Fossland*   142

VII MOMENTS OF TRUTH

We Are All Connected   *Jean Wenzel*   147

The "Write" Match   *Alice Stern Weiser*   149

Leading from the Heart   *Holly Esparza*   151

My Sailor Man   *Linda Ross Swanson*   154

Feedback Is a Gift   *Diane Ripstein*   157

Rhymes and Reasons   *Antionette Vigliaturo Ishmael*   160

It's All in the Frijoles   *Yolanda Nava*   162

Something to Chew On   *Rita Davenport*   165

VIII THE ANIMAL CONNECTION

One Soul, Two Halves   *Ellen Urbani Hiltebrand*   171

Keeping the High Watch   *Eileen Davis*   176

Dazy Joy   *Cindy Potter*   178

Oscar   *Cindy Hanson*   180

Look-Alike Lucys   *Susan Miles*   182

A Flutter of Butterfly Wings   *Lon My Lam*   184

A Gift of Love   *Debb Janes*   186

IX ACTS OF KINDNESS

The Memory Jar   *Mary LoVerde*   191

Road Warriors   *Ann Benson*   193

For the Love of Students   *Emory Austin*   196

Love Notes   *Debra Ayers Brown*   198

Surrogate Dreamer   *Marlene L. King*   201

Special Delivery   *Lisa Juscik*   204

Rituals That Touch the Heart   *Kay Allenbaugh*   206

Lesson for a Lifetime   *Sheila S. Hudson*   208

X A DEEPER REFLECTION

Four Weddings and a Miracle   *Kate McKern Verigin*   213

Does the Breast Have a Soul?   *Lynne Massie*   217

All That Glitters   *Mary Carroll-Hackett*   220

A New Deal   *Burky Achilles*   222

Entrances and Exits   *Linda G. Engel*   225

For Betty   *Tammy Kling*   228

United States of Motherhood   *Joanna Slan*   230

XI
SERIOUSLY FUNNY

A Streak of Love   *Carole Bellacera*   235

Venus Rising   *Carmen D'Amico*   237

When Will I Be Thin?   *Maureen Gorsuch*   239

The Great Zucchini Caper   *Karyn Buxman*   240

Warranty X   *Ann E. Weeks*   245

The Purple People   *Jennifer Howard*   246

A Christmas Surprise Indeed!   *Roberta B. Jacobson*   248

More Chocolate Stories?   249

Contributors   251

Acknowledgments   269

Permissions Acknowledgments   270

> "The heart that breaks open can contain the whole universe.
> Your heart is that large. Trust it. Keep breathing."
> —Joanna Macy

INTRODUCTION

Inspirational stories feed our souls and give life to our dreams. They help us to take our next important step as we learn and grow. I am honored that seventy-four dynamic women have shared their favorite personal stories in *Chocolate for a Woman's Heart*. Many of the writers in this book are motivational speakers, spiritual leaders, consultants, therapists, and best-selling authors, and their work influences audiences around the country. You will laugh and cry but never forget the powerful stories they share. Who better to warm your heart than women who are dedicated to uplifting and encouraging others? With a loving hand, I gratefully extend these stories to you.

Regardless of your own uniqueness, you will find a common thread that runs through all women's lives; and it is that shared experience that we've set out to capture in *Chocolate for a Woman's Heart*. Some of these real-life stories will give you just the lift you need, while others will be perfect for your best friend, mother, or daughter. All the stories honor and celebrate a woman's desire to love, nurture, and give from her heart—when it's easy and during the most difficult times.

Why chocolate? Women and chocolate are made for each other. Women have never needed science to tell us that chocolate creates those "feel-good" endorphins in our bodies. Just like the rich taste of chocolate, the stories in *Chocolate for a Woman's Heart* will bring you a warm sense of satisfaction deep down inside. You can almost taste the love that abounds within these pages, the thought-provoking moments of truth.

Chocolate for a Woman's Heart is, I feel, a divinely inspired project and is a sequel to my first book, *Chocolate for a Woman's Soul*. I've since learned that compiling these books has a lot to do with addressing my own courage issues. I have always had a fear of public speaking. If I had simply taken baby steps through that fear earlier on in my life, I would not have felt such anxiety when it came to promoting *Chocolate for a Woman's Soul*. With its enormous success, I found myself having to walk through a lifelong fear before I could join in the celebration. I hope the stories in *Chocolate for a Woman's Heart* will nudge, encourage, and move you to walk through your own fears, follow your intuition, discover love, and identify your personal beauty and magnificence.

I learned a lot about myself in writing and compiling these heartfelt stories. My desire is that the stories will affect your life as positively as they have affected mine. Indulge in their richness as you explore the wide range of experiences within the varied chapters of *Chocolate for a Woman's Heart*. Pick the perfect story daily—knowing you'll get the soul-satisfying lift you need to discover your heart's desires!

I
DIVINE INTERVENTION

*"You block your dream
when you allow your fear
to grow bigger than your faith."*

—Mary Manin Morrissey

BACK-SEAT DRIVER

My father died when I was ten years old. I used to wake up and hear my mother crying. Angry at my father for dying, I told myself that I would never get married and let a man hurt me like my mother was hurting.

Life went on. As I grew older, my youth leaders said that I would grow up and find a young man whom I would want to marry. The hurt from my father's death was still too fresh for me to take that prediction to heart.

One night in prayer, I explored my strong feeling that I didn't think I could ever let myself love someone who could hurt me. If I was intended to marry, how could I lower my barriers enough to be receptive? As I prayed, I asked for help. I felt a great calm and peace come over me.

After graduating from high school, I went to the University of Arizona. Coming home from a party, a nice young man offered me a ride. I knew him only through mutual friends. We were getting acquainted through small talk when we pulled up to a stoplight.

"This is the man you will marry!" a voice from the back seat said. I turned around to see who was sitting in the back. No one was there.

"Did you just hear someone?" I asked my companion. "No," he replied.

I continued to think about what I'd heard. I realized it was an answer to my prayer so very long ago!

Eight months later, I married that young man. We have been married twenty-four years and have six beautiful children.

I still marvel that my childhood prayer was answered like

clockwork at the perfect moment. I heard one more comment from the "back seat" that fateful night. The Divine voice said, "You asked me to tell you."

ANAMAE ELLEDGE

A DREAM COME TRUE

*F*ollowing World War II, I was living the American dream—a cozy cottage, Betty Crocker in the kitchen, rambling roses on the picket fence, a baby carriage in the nursery, a savings account, and Gold Bond stamps.

In the early stages of my second pregnancy, nasty telltale signs of impending trouble appeared one afternoon. I began bleeding heavily, and my doctor advised me to get myself immediately to the hospital, where he would meet me.

When I was propped up in the strange comfort of my hospital bed, my feet raised high and cold packs resting on my belly, Dr. Weiker told me he would wait for the lab report and decide on a plan of action the following morning. With a reassuring smile and friendly wishes for a good night, he left. Soon after that, my husband, edgy and nervous, went home to take care of our little boy.

Left to myself in the quiet of my cheerful hospital room, I speculated on what was happening in my body and wondered if I would lose the baby whose living presence I already loved and cherished. I forced myself to concentrate on stilling my worries and dwelling on only that which would be best for the baby. The dark night sky closed in on my room as I drifted peacefully off to sleep, ready for dreams to tell me a story.

An image of a small summer garden appeared in a dream. It was ablaze with tall white daisies and dazzling snapdragons. Blue skies and dappled sunlight enhanced the colors of the flowers. Just then a tiny girl came into my vision and walked toward me. She had soft golden-brown curls and light-brown eyes set wide apart in a round, adorable face. She was dressed in a white-and-blue gingham dress, with a white piqué Peter Pan collar and narrow white cuffs on puffed sleeves. The letters *ABC* were embroidered in bold bright-red yarn across the top of her dress. Suddenly her little face took on a sad expression, and from her rosebud mouth there issued a bell-like voice. "Mommy, Mommy, don't let them take me away from you!" she pleaded.

Voiceless, I screamed, unable to stop until I awoke—a hand on my shoulder gently shaking me back into reality. The kind face of a nurse loomed over me. "Don't be afraid," she said in a soothing voice. "Everything will be all right. Go back to sleep. No more nightmares. Good night."

I nodded sleepily and obediently closed my eyes, holding the vision of the little girl in my mind. No sooner had I drifted back into sleep than I found myself in the garden once more, and the tiny girl once again transfixed me with her eyes. She pleaded shrilly, "Mommy, Mommy! Don't let them take me away from you!"

That time I woke up to my own shouting, which soon turned to tears and a few moments of uncontrolled sobbing. Once again the nurse appeared, put her arms around me, and quietly talked me back into the peaceful quiet of my room. Dawn came slowly, erasing the shadows of the dark night and filling me with a sense of purpose and a strange knowing of untold secrets.

My doctor appeared early in the morning, all dressed in surgical greens, a mask dangling from his handsome face. "All set for the D and C," he announced. "The lab reports indicated you've miscarried. We'll clean you out, and in three months you can start thinking again about having a baby," he concluded, matter-of-factly.

"I'm pregnant," I announced. "I'm not going to have a D and C, and furthermore," I added triumphantly, "I'm going to have a little girl in seven months."

He looked at me in surprise, remarking that he'd always thought I was a sensible, rational person with both feet on the ground. I should put fanciful thoughts out of my mind and get on with my life. We argued back and forth for quite a while, until finally he gave in to my request for a new pregnancy test before hauling me off to the operating room. He departed with an injured air to the set of his squared shoulders. I went back to sleep.

Several hours later, he walked into my room, no longer dressed in greens. He stood at the foot of my bed, shaking his head, and said, "Well, you were right! You *are* pregnant. You must have aborted a twin."

When I answered his question as to how I knew I was pregnant, he looked even more puzzled than during our previous argument. He shook his head, gave me a hug, and left. I suppose what I told him—my dreams of a little girl—was just too much for his scientific mind and medical training. I never told my story to anyone else, but I promised myself that one day I would tell it to my daughter. I was quite certain I would have a girl!

Seven months later, almost to the day, I gave birth to a healthy little baby girl, with a tiny round face and golden fuzz for hair. My doctor could only shake his head again and, in a somewhat exasperated tone of voice, mumble something under his breath about "Women . . . their dreams . . . their intuition . . . their spooky ways."

Happily, I took my daughter home, marveling at her light-brown eyes, which seemed to stay locked onto mine, telling me things I needed to know.

The first baby present to arrive in the mail was sent by a good friend of mine who lived in New York City. She knew nothing about the circumstances of my daughter's birth. When I opened the gaily wrapped box and gently parted the protective layers of crisp tissue paper, I lifted out a white-and-blue gingham dress with a white piqué Peter Pan collar and white cuffs on puffed sleeves. The letters *ABC* were embroidered in bold bright-red yarn across the top.

URSULA BACON

SMALL MIRACLES

*I*t was a breathless July day. Humidity clung in foggy clouds on windows and dripped down perspiring foreheads. In sauna-like conditions, the annual baseball playoff game was in progress. Anxious parents stuck to metal bleachers, and tension escalated as the championship game approached.

Adam was the littlest guy on his team. All season, he'd been hitless. Sitting on the bench gave him time to think about things and to remember his big brother Neal, his hero.

Four summers earlier, Neal had died in an accident. Adam missed him, especially now with his team needing help. He wished his big brother were here to root him on.

Adam's team was behind 5–4 with two outs as the game drew to a close. When Adam heard his name called, he walked hesitantly up to bat. The outfielders moved in when they saw the little batter step up to the plate. Adam swung at the first pitch. "Stee-rike one!" called out the umpire. The second wobbly swing brought "Stee-rike two!" Hope dwindled as fans and teammates gathered their things to leave.

But wait! Hold everything! Our hearts were in our throats as we noticed something happening with Adam. A look of confidence crossed his face as he gripped the bat, waiting for the final pitch. Was it the spirit of his brother encouraging him on? Was it Adam wanting to show Neal he could do it? In that magical moment, Adam's third swing connected with the ball! He quickly found himself standing on first base, dazed and triumphant. Fans and teammates jumped to their feet, cheering! Maybe Neal was there after all!

That's all it took to get the team fired up. Encouraged by Adam's moment of glory, the next few batters got hits also. Soon Adam touched home plate with the winning run. The moment he crossed the plate, the crowd heard Adam yell "Yes!"

The little guy with big courage taught us some important life lessons:

- *Yes* to small miracles!
- *Yes* to heroes and the example they set!
- *Yes* to never giving up!
- *Yes* to stepping up to bat in life!

JILL AND CANDIS FANCHER

A WISE MAN, A MENTOR, OR AN ANGEL?

My hands rushed to my face, and I sobbed with joy. After five attempts, I had finally won the title of Miss Hawaii. Flashbulbs flickered like little lightning bolts, congratulations echoed from the crowd. After the festivities had wound down, I headed to my dressing room, alone. I saw him then. A man in his forties with a quiet, kind face, dressed in bland colors and smoking a pipe. He was portly, with gentle brown eyes framed by eyeglasses and wispy hair combed straight back. The aroma of his cherry pipe tobacco was instantly comforting.

"Congratulations! You deserved to win," he said.

How did he know that? "Who are you?"

"My name is George." His smile disappeared, and his eyes turned serious. "We need to talk, Donna. Ten o'clock tomorrow at the coffee shop."

I was tempted to laugh at first, but my curiosity won out. He wasn't menacing, just sure of himself. I nodded yes.

"I sensed your hesitation, and I do intend to justify my actions by passing on a message to you."

"OK—let's hear it."

"To fulfill your destiny, Donna, you must leave the Hawaiian Islands next year."

This time I couldn't help laughing. "I love it here."

George sighed. "All right, then, you leave me no choice but to predict three incidents that will occur before we have breakfast tomorrow."

Now what? I thought, and opened my mouth to speak, but George put up his hand.

"Your car will be towed, your kitchen's leaky pipes will burst, and the noiseless third step in your apartment will begin to creak."

By the next morning, everything George predicted had happened. My car wouldn't start, my roommate was in tears because the kitchen pipes were leaking badly, and as I climbed the stairs to my room, I heard a creaking sound, which came from the third step. Over breakfast, I asked how he knew so much about me.

I thought I detected a squint in one eye as he smiled. "We rarely listen to our intuition—our inner voice that tells us what to do. For instance, I know I'm supposed to be in your life, to watch over you and be around when you need me. You must now search for your own truth."

And search I did. I went on to compete in the Miss USA pageant in Miami and lost. The next year I moved to Los Angeles, and I struggled for seven years to become an actress. Meanwhile, George and I talked frequently on the phone or met when he came to L.A. Trying to stay thin and beautiful, I became bulimic and hooked on diet pills. I was alone and miserable, and contemplating suicide, when the phone rang. It was George. He said, "You've got a lot of work to do. Don't you dare think about checking out."

"How did you know?" I asked, dumbfounded.

"I'm leaving Oklahoma. I'll be in L.A. this afternoon, and then we'll talk."

That day, George convinced me to believe in myself again. "Your life will change at thirty. Hang in there for a few more years."

Age thirty sailed in, and I still wanted off this earth. I had hit rock bottom—emotionally, financially, spiritually, and mentally. On March 1, 1978, I boarded a DC-10 from Los Angeles to Hawaii, to emcee a Miss Hawaii pageant. The plane exploded on takeoff, and I was the last to escape the rear section of the flaming aircraft. Transported to a medical triage, I asked where the nearest phone was. This time I called George.

He said, "It has changed, Donna. You can finally see the big picture. It's time to get out of your own way—time to help others."

I didn't understand completely, but I ended up waiving my right to sue the airline and became an envoy for the dead and burned passengers. I fought for better safety regulations and was grilled in court for hours by the big guns representing the airline. After it was over, I stepped down from the witness stand, drained and again alone. When I reached the courthouse parking lot, George was leaning against my car, smoking his pipe.

"I just got to town," he said. "Let's get an ice cream and walk on the sand."

Watching the sun set over Santa Monica Beach, I babbled countless questions and George patiently answered every one. I felt restored by his philosophy, insight, and truth.

"Understand," he said, "we all have fears, but our destiny is to conquer them." I knew at that moment that I would go on to teach survival skills.

"George, please tell me," I begged, "will I marry, have children, and be happy?"

He looked out over the sea and spoke in measured words. "You'll have a daughter late in life, and oh, yeah, she'll be a pistol. She'll have your energy and will be a leader. The bonding between you and your daughter will be miraculous." A smile lit up his face. "And, Donna, she'll come to you."

"What exactly do you mean by that?" I asked.

"The truth is inside you. Trust yourself. Pursue your destiny with power."

It was later that I learned I was not destined to give birth. I put in for an adoption, only to be overlooked by the birth mothers year after year. I worried that single moms over forty were not on their agenda.

George passed away suddenly, from cancer. I was devastated. I never got to say good-bye. The last time I spoke to him, George had said, "Your daughter is coming—and I'll be there."

Three more years passed before I got a call from Las Vegas. My prayers had been answered. I was ecstatic. A birth mother and father chose me. I had six short weeks to deal with the mounds of paperwork required for the adoption.

I named my baby Mariah. Seventy-two hours after her birth, the final papers were ready to sign. The birth mother was pushing Mariah in her bassinet down the brightly lit hospital corridor, and she said indignantly, "I smell pipe smoke. Can you imagine that—and in a baby nursery?" My heart flip-flopped and I was frozen to the spot as I watched her dart from room to room, searching for the offender. When she returned, she said, "That's odd—there's no one here. I know I smelled cherry tobacco. Did you?"

Tears welled up in my eyes and streamed down my cheeks. "Yes."

"Donna, what's wrong?" she asked.

"I don't know if you believe in the spiritual world, but there was a man named George who was always there for me in my times of great need. He told me years ago, just before he died, I would have a daughter and he'd be here when that happened. George smoked cherry tobacco in his pipe."

My birth mother stared at me wide-eyed and said, "I chose you because I feel this child is going to become a leader and I can't give her what she needs, but you can."

She bent over the bassinet and lifted the baby up to me. I smiled down at Mariah and murmured to her, "What do you think, darling? Was George a wise man, a mentor, or an angel?"

DONNA HARTLEY

TURNING POINT

There's a very fine line between having a nightmare and having a dream.

Cruising along Interstate 55, Mom and Dad were on their way to a trailer show in St. Louis. At one point, they were following a motor home. As a long time RVer, Dad sees things on the road that others don't see. "That motor home isn't tracking properly," he said to my mom. "There's a slight wobble in the left rear wheel."

Knowing how dangerous a loose wheel could be, and fearing the worst, he decided to alert the driver. He pulled toward the front of the motor home and said, "Rose, why don't you get the driver's attention? See if you can get them to pull over." Mom began to wave at the woman driving the motor home and to point toward the rear of her RV. The woman ignored her.

A bit frustrated by the woman's refusal to respond, Dad considered it might not be worth the effort to get them to stop. He dropped back to take another look at their rear wheel, and shook his head. "That's not safe. Their wheel could fall off and the motor home would tip over. At sixty mph, it would kill them. If I have to, I'll run them off the road."

As providence would have it, there was a truck weigh station just ahead. If it was necessary to run someone off the road, Dad knew this would be the place to do it. He drove his car closer and closer to the motor home, honking his horn, while Mom motioned to the driver to pull over. The woman had little choice but to comply.

Dad stopped the car to get out. Now he was the one in danger. Running a stranger off the road simply isn't a wise thing to do in the nineties. Mom said, "It might be better if I get out with you, dear. We'll appear less threatening that way." By now the man on the passenger side of the motor home, who had been sleeping, was walking toward Dad. Pointing to Mom and Dad, his wife said, "Those people just ran us off the road."

Dad, keeping his distance, raised his hands where they could be seen. He said, "You might be pretty angry for what I just did. I'm an RVer too. I know I'd be angry. Before you do anything, just walk to the back of your motor home and take a look at your left rear wheel."

Not quite knowing what to make of my folks, the man walked with some hesitation toward the back of his motor home. He looked at the wheel, then removed the hubcap. Two lug nuts fell to the ground. Realizing the wheel had been close to falling off, he was visibly shaken. He walked up front and told his wife about the possible disaster they had just avoided.

She burst into tears and hugged both my parents, clinging tight. Finally able to talk, she said, "Last night I dreamed that I was driving down the road and lost control of our motor home. It began weaving back and forth wildly. I shouted to my husband, and he turned to me just as we began to roll over. I woke up with a start and lay in bed shaking, because it had seemed so real."

My dad had demonstrated that if we pay attention, each of us has opportunities daily to divinely influence the lives around us.

Seize those opportunities.

Thwart nightmares.

Be a dream weaver.

REV. DEBORAH OLIVE

DIVINE ASSISTANCE

Several years ago, I visited a young mother at home. The doctors said she had just a few days to live, as the cancer she had battled so courageously had advanced throughout her body.

Seeing her during those last days had been particularly hard for me. Sally was one of the most beautiful people I have ever experienced. Long before she had cancer, I remember watching Sally leave church one Sunday morning and thinking: She is too gentle for this world. She had a purity about her.

Dealing with her cancer was the fight of her life. She had done everything that her church teaches. She had done everything she learned in her Native American tradition. She had done everything that medical science offered her—surgery, chemotherapy, radiation, and even a bone marrow transplant. Nothing stopped the cancer. Sally began to accept that she would soon make her transition.

I remember getting ready to go visit her to say good-bye and be with her. It was a very hard thing for me to do. While putting my makeup on, I heard a voice say, "Tell her about the angels." And I immediately said, "No way! She doesn't want to hear that. She's already pretty angry as it is."

While I drove to her home, that voice kept saying, "You tell her about the angels." And I thought: I will not. Yes, I talk to angels, but I've never seen one. I'm not going to tell her about the angels this morning.

Having made that decision, I walked into her home. And it happened. Even though the lights were dimmed, the room glowed with a brilliant radiance—a radiance that had no apparent source. I had never been in so awesome a presence! I went to my knees the moment I walked into that room. I didn't think, I just went down in honor and respect. All my resistance against speaking of angels vanished.

Sitting there in silence, I felt an absolute sense of peace. Sally looked over at me, and I saw anger in her eyes. She asked me, "Why?" That's a tough question to answer for a dying woman in the prime of her life, with two beautiful sons and a husband she cherished.

I told her the only truth I knew: "I don't know. I do not know. But I need to tell you something very important. When you're ready to make your transition, the angels will come for you, and your most beloved relatives will be there with you. You don't have to be afraid. You will see a great light."

She looked over at me, and the anger disappeared. Her face became as radiant as the room. "Then it's begun," she whispered. "It's already started." And she went back into peaceful silence.

At Sally's memorial service, I shared with her relatives my reluctance to tell her about the angels. "Well, maybe we should tell you what happened while you were visiting Sally that morning," one of them responded. They had left Sally alone for a few hours, knowing I was coming. While they ate lunch at the kitchen table, a garbage truck went by, making its regular pickups. They noticed that something fell off the back as the truck drove off. Out of curiosity, they went outside to see what it was.

What they found was as powerful as Sally's illuminated room. What they found reinforced the persistent message I'd heard while getting ready to see Sally for the last time. What they found convinced me of what I knew but could not see. The book that fell out of the passing garbage truck was titled *Angels on Assignment*.

REV. MARY OMWAKE

> *"Women never have young minds.*
> *They are born three thousand years old."*
> —SHELAGH DELANY

EARTH ANGEL

I teach Reiki, an ancient system of hands-on healing. In the advanced classes, I instruct my students to send healing energy to others at a distance, or even backward in time. Esoteric concepts to be sure, but nonetheless quite possible.

While driving through Montana with a friend on our way to a seminar, I was lost in thought as I watched one rolling hill after another melt into the overcast sky. There were few cars on the open road, so we were surprised to see the flashing lights up ahead in the distance. "Oh, no, an accident," I said to myself. We slowed down, and as we passed the scene of chaos I gasped. A car had rolled over completely, and its contents were strewn all over the grass lining the highway. Paramedics were just lifting a person on a stretcher into the ambulance. "Dear God," I prayed, "please help them." I remembered my Reiki training and started to send healing energy back in time to arrive at the moment of the accident. I prayed that my work might have some good effect.

All of a sudden, I felt the familiar sensations of healing energy running up and down my spine, much stronger than ever before. It was as if I had been plugged into a light socket, the electrical sensations were so intense. I'm lucky my friend is driving, I thought. Seconds later, my eyelids became heavy and my head slumped forward as I slipped into a dreamlike state. In this condition of altered awareness, I went back in time, watching the car roll. Immediately, as if someone had hit Rewind on the scene, I was in spirit form, inside the car, moments before the vehicle careened out of control. I felt a sickening lunge as the car began to flip. In my spirit form, I held the woman as she rolled and held her closer as the car rolled again. Infinite tenderness and love seemed to flow through me and out of my hands.

My awareness shifted back to the car I was riding in. I felt a tremendous heat flaming through my abdomen and in the small of my back. "Feel this," I mumbled to my friend. He reached over and put his hand on my back. "Wow!" He kept driving as I slipped back into the "dream."

I heard a voice echoing as if we were underwater. The voice became clearer. "This is her sister. Tell her I love her." I felt a huge presence of love flow through my heart and course through my veins. The moment of altered awareness ended, and I burst back into the present time.

Something transformational had happened within me. Tears of joy welled up in me, so great had been the love I'd just felt. By now we were miles past the accident. "She's OK," I told my friend as I dried my eyes. I just knew.

We arrived at a beautiful ranch nestled in an old pine forest, where we would be studying a Native American perspective on healing and living in balance. I became absorbed in the workshop activities, as the incident on the road faded into a memory. Two days into the seminar, however, a remarkable announcement was made by the seminar leader. "We are pleased to announce," the facilitator said, "that one of your fellow students will soon be joining you. Janine was in a bad accident on her way here." I stopped eating. With my fork still in midair, I listened intently. "Her car rolled over two and a half times, but miraculously she was unhurt. She has only minor cuts and some bad bruises." "My God," I said to myself. "She's the one."

When I introduced myself to Janine, I held back tears and told her what I'd "seen." Somewhat shyly—because I didn't know how she'd take it—I mentioned the message from her sister. She looked at me, her eyes widening. "I felt like angel hands were holding me," she said simply. "And yes, my sister did pass away some time ago. I've always felt she was with me." We looked into each other's eyes, soul-to-soul and saw the connection that bridges time and space.

Some things defy explanation and logic. Sometimes we just intuitively know. Down to my core, I know that my prayer was answered. I had a special opportunity to influence and protect the life of another being. I got to experience the profound honor of momentarily being an earth angel.

Ann Albers

> *"Change doesn't happen in the middle.
> It only happens when we venture over to the edge
> and take one small step after another."*
> —Karen Sheridan

OUR TEACHERS COME IN MANY FORMS

Our chauffeured bus meandered lazily along the country road, heading to a vineyard for a charity auction to benefit the Salvation Army. A group of us from a local business club rode together. Looking out the window to watch the sun peeking through the continuous stream of birch and maple trees was relaxing.

The low hum of many private conversations could be heard throughout the bus. My husband, Eric, and our friend Phyllis and I were huddled together in the back. Our exchanges quickly went from casual conversation to "How are you *really?*"

I found myself once again pouring out my fear of public speaking. With my first book about to be published, I knew it was my job to publicly promote it. I questioned why I had put myself in this predicament. My book included inspirational stories from speakers around the country—women who couldn't wait to get in front of a group and empower others. I thought they were the natural ones to talk with the media, sharing their uplifting messages from the book, thus letting me off the hook. But God had a bigger vision for me! It was as if He had played a joke on me. In reality, the author needs to be "out there" speaking to groups too. Listening to His guidance had taken me this far down the path, and now there was no turning back. I had to grow!

Aware of my inner struggle, Phyllis pulled out a small velvet bag, loosened the tassel bow, and told me to reach in and choose a card at random. The affirmation card I selected read: *"Breakthrough . . . You will be changed at depth . . . You will not recognize yourself."* We laughed, yet we wondered about the message. Was a big change coming my way? Did I hold any stock in this process? We nestled back in our seats, keeping our thoughts to ourselves.

At that moment, I felt a power surge in my heart. It was a distinct physical sensation of being filled up. "It's the craziest thing!" I told Phyllis. "My body feels like it just got a dose of confidence!"

An hour later, at the vineyard, we sat at picnic tables covered with red-and-white checkered tablecloths and ate our box lunches. The coordinator of the event introduced the fund-raising auctioneer.

The bidding for a case of Merlot wine was going at a snail's pace when my husband shouted out to the auctioneer, "I'll give you one hundred dollars."

With no response from the quiet crowd, I shouted out, "I'll give you two hundred dollars." My confident tone surprised both me and Eric. The crowd roared as they observed our banter as we competed for the same case of wine.

"We're in this together, babe," Eric said with a laugh. But my enthusiasm to use my newfound voice could not be contained. We got ourselves a case of wine for far more than we needed to pay for it.

The auctioneer pulled me up front with him, knowing my enthusiasm would be contagious to potential bidders. I found myself speaking with and leading a group that had become responsive to my spontaneity. The bidding back and forth increased and influenced others to give to a good cause. Where had this new freedom come from—not only to speak but to shout in joy in front of a group? I believe I was being shown that I could indeed do what I feared I could not. It was as if God was saying, "Your fear of speaking is not serving you well. I'm always here to support you. Release the fear, and go forward in joy."

Our teachers come in many forms. It's amazing what happens when we put ourselves in an open, learning, receptive mode. Selecting an affirmation card felt unfamiliar, yet the "perfect" message I got was just the boost I needed to learn and grow.

You see, God filled me up right where I was. I may not always hear an important message in the most conventional way. The lyrics in a song on the radio may give me what I need at a special time. Or the words in a greeting card from a friend may inspire me. A powerful quote from an ancient teacher may stir my soul, or I may discover my next life step as the wind brushes my cheek while I hike in the woods.

With many radio and TV shows behind me, amazing things have happened since that turning point when I stepped through the doorway of fear into a world of trust. I now remember God's words to us all: "If you knew who walked with you, how could you be afraid?"

KAY ALLENBAUGH

II
GROWTH SPURTS

"Like yourself now. Be ten years ahead of your friends."
—Jennifer James

"There is no power on earth that can withstand the power of love. By loving our enemies we turn them into friends."
—STELLA TERRILL MANN

ANGEL OF THE LORD

I kept an eye on the disheveled young man dressed in black leather who stood near the chapel. As a security guard for a hospital in Georgia, I checked people out, particularly those who looked suspicious. When I asked this young man if I could help him, he told me he was waiting for someone. I made a mental note to keep close tabs on him. Returning later to look for him, I found him gone.

A while later, I patrolled the hospital corridors and saw that young man fast asleep on a pew in the chapel. He no longer looked to be a threat. He looked like a wet puppy brought in from the cold November day. As I watched him sleep, I remembered what my mom had told me as a child: "No matter who you come in contact with, no matter how ragged they look, treat them kindly—they could be an angel of the Lord."

I asked Easter, my co-worker and friend, to help me. We dug in our purses, pooled our change, and bought a lunch from the cafeteria for this shabby stranger. I set the food tray beside him, tucked a pillow under his head, and covered him with a blanket—careful not to wake him.

When he awoke the next morning, I had gone home from work. He found Easter and asked her who had been so kind to him the night before. He was surprised to learn that this act of kindness had come from a black security guard.

His expression was one of despair and confusion as he confessed, "I've never been around a black person before. Everything my friends taught me about blacks is untrue. I was told they are out to cut your throat. That doesn't make sense. I've got to sort out some things."

Because of our special encounter, we each got to see each other with acceptance rather than judgment. For this young man to recognize me as a person and for me to recognize his need for compassion changed both our lives forever. A moment of healing allowed us never to see things as we did before. This experience caused me to ask, "What if we looked upon each person we met as an angel of the Lord?"

You never know when an act of kindness will draw people together. With some apprehension, this scruffy stranger took off his worn jacket, rolled up his shirtsleeve, and revealed to Easter a startling tattoo symbolizing who he used to be. It read: *Ku Klux Klan*.

ARLINE CRAWFORD BURTON

JUST A HAIR MORE LOVE

*I*always had a difficult relationship with the wavy, thick patch of black that crowned my small head like a jester's hat. Footloose and free-spirited, it chose a new course with each sunrise. It tumbled down my forehead one day and curled cavalierly backward the next. I should have loved its impetuous nature, its fearless embrace of change, its sparkle and shine. Instead I have done battle with my hair for almost four decades, shamelessly attempting to break the spirit of those now silver-streaked locks. Despite endless coaxing, cajoling, and threats, I could never get those wild things to work together to produce what could be viewed as a hair style. Bereft of all hope, I yielded smoldering dissatisfaction to outright disdain for my hair.

I, who always believed in the underdog . . . I, who still gave loose change to men wandering skid row . . . I, who woke up smiling with the conviction that every day offered new promise . . . I, who bought cookies, candy bars, wrapping paper and losing raffle tickets from every child who rang the doorbell . . . I, who thought my earnest study of various spiritual traditions testified to my personal evolution—I could not love my own hair.

In desperation, I began to meditate about it. I burned incense. I held a smudging ceremony in my bathroom. I knelt before the Hair Goddess and begged for mercy. Then it happened—a pure and direct connection to the Divine. The Hair Goddess spoke:

My child, long have I waited for you. Coveting thy neighbor's hair is wrong. Hair spray, mousse, and the blow dryer are all false gods. Inner peace and wisdom are attained by honoring the wildness of your hair. Do not resist it; embrace it.

With that the Hair Goddess faded. I called out to her, but she said no more. And so I began the long journey toward loving my hair. When I got frustrated, I apologized; when I flew into a rage and scowled in the mirror, I put myself in time out. Within a year's time I was having a love affair with my hair. I had a sophisticated hairstyle, and I reveled in the compliments I received.

One day I went to my usual salon for a little trim, and something went terribly wrong. Despite my instructions, my perfect hairstyle was snipped into thousands of lost locks on the floor. Too upset to speak, I drove home in a daze. Tears in my eyes, I knelt once more before the great Hair Goddess, seeking solace and answers. The goddess appeared and kissed me gently on the forehead. A smile began to play upon her lips, and she spoke: "This was only a test. Had this been a real hair emergency, you would have had a job interview tomorrow."

O. C. O'CONNELL

SOULMATING

When my son, Ryan, went off to college, I was confident I had instilled in him the qualities that would prepare him to be a good citizen of the world. Then I held my breath. Kids were kids. It was his first taste of freedom. He was going to screw up. It was inevitable.

I had no time for the "empty nest syndrome." I was preparing my lines for the kinds of calls we children of the sixties and seventies gave our parents. "Hiya, Ma! I'm in jail. . . . But it was just beer! They said it was legal on campus!" Stuff like that.

Two weeks later, Ryan came home to Houston, laundry bag in hand. When I asked him how he found college—other than filthy, judging from the amount of dirty clothes he had—he said, "Well, you know, Mom, there are some really, really weird people on campus."

I imagined perverts, druggies, gangsta-type seniors, HIV-positive coeds pursuing their MRS. I asked, "Like how weird?"

"Like nutzoid. Mike and Carl and I went over to Darcy's room to meet her roommate and some other freshman girls. We were all crammed in this room and talking, and this one girl starts singing! Bursts into song. Not soft, but loud. Like kinda drowning out what we were trying to say. It was weird."

"The songs were weird?"

"No, *she* was weird. She wouldn't give it a rest, either. She would just keep humming to herself, even while we were talking."

"Where was she from?"

"Houston. And she didn't even know her roommate, Mom! She was assigned to her room."

"Imagine that!" I said, remembering my own experience (wasn't that just last week?), when *all* our roommates were strangers.

"What kind of person wouldn't hand-pick their roommate?"

At this point I'm getting an uneasy feeling. He's acting a bit too assertive and sheepishly avoids eye contact.

"Ryan, by any chance did you make fun of that girl?"

Silence.

My skin crawled with goose bumps, and suddenly I envisioned myself in that room with those kids. I felt I knew them all, except for the singing girl. I certainly knew the razor-keen sense of humor my son possessed. He could give Robin Williams a run for his money. I felt the pain, embarrassment, and loneliness of the singing girl.

There were tears in my eyes. "Ryan, you've always been too picky about people. I think you said something to hurt this girl. Something that maybe didn't seem like much to you but to her was biting and dreadful. The minute you get back to campus, I want you to find that girl, and you apologize to her."

"Aw, Ma . . ."

Ryan went back to school on Sunday night, and he called me the next night. "Mom, you know the singing girl? She's gone! Her roommate told me that she left campus. Dropped out! Went back home and enrolled at the University of Houston. It's all my fault, Mom. I just know I hurt her, like you said."

The year passed, and Ryan came home from college, older and wiser. That summer, he worked long hours doing hard labor for his father and me in our swimming pool and spa business.

He and the crew delivered a spa to one of our customers, who telephoned my husband later that day and said, "My daughter saw a young man delivering our spa, and she would like to go out with him, but she's too shy to ask. Could you tell me who the tall blond boy is?"

"My son," my husband answered. "I'll be happy to pass along the message."

Ryan was puzzled. "I never saw a girl there. But I do remember somebody watching through the curtains at the bedroom window. Maybe that was her."

Ryan, who liked to make new friends, called Christy and

made a date. The following Saturday night, after meeting her parents, he walked Christy to his car. When they were about to pull away from the curb, Ryan turned to her and said, "You were the singing girl in Darcy's room."

"Yes, Ryan, I was."

"I'm so sorry for how I treated you."

"I know you are, Ryan."

When Ryan came home that night and told me the story, we both had tears in our eyes. I was flooded with that incredible feeling I get when I know my life has been divinely touched.

I looked at my son and said, "Ryan, you're going to marry that girl someday."

"I know, Mom," he said—and he did, several years later.

Of all the joys in my life, knowing that my son found his soul mate is the greatest of them all.

Just think if Ryan had not budged from his first impression. It reminded me of the saying I shared with him when this whole episode started: "Be careful," I had said. *"What you focus on determines what you miss!"*

CATHERINE LANIGAN

*"I think the one lesson I have learned
is that there is no substitute for paying attention."*
—Diane Sawyer

MOVING THE MOON

I was sitting under a sycamore tree, reading, one late afternoon, while my daughter, too young to be a swimmer, wandered back and forth on the top steps of our pool. Suddenly she called out, "Mom, look! The moon!"

Wanting to be left to my reading, I said in a tone that I hoped conveyed this, "Honey, I can't see it from under this tree."

"That's okay," she said. "I'll move it so you can."

Move the moon? She had my attention. She began walking across the pool steps and, from her perspective, pulled the moon away from the tree.

"The moon follows me," she confided matter-of-factly.

Now, fully aware that this was one of those magic moments of motherhood, I closed the book and walked out from under the tree.

"Yes, I can see it now."

It was beautiful in the almost evening light—a near-full moon with one blurred edge.

"Thank you for showing me the moon," I said, and meant it.

"Why does the moon follow me?" she said, with the pleased self-assurance of a starlet.

I paused and reflected before I answered. With my first child, I would have rattled off scientific facts about perspective and perception. If my second child had asked about the moon following him, I would have said, "I knew that answer once. I think I remember where to look it up. I'll make a note of it. I'll get back with you on that."

But this child, this magic fairy being, who *knows* the moon is following *her*—what do I say to her? I knew that soon enough someone (probably a brother) would inform her roughly that the moon does *not* follow her. Or in the slow brutality of growing up it would gradually seep into her awareness that the moon couldn't be following her. And as she moved into adulthood, she would forget she had that magic and at some point, like me, forget all about the moon and even stop looking at it.

"Look! I'm making it jump up and down. See it?" she called out anew.

I was still in a reverie. Then—I am ashamed to admit it, but it happens to us mothers occasionally—I had a momentary lapse. After all, she was interrupting my great train of thought. She was saying, "Did you see me make the moon jump up and down?" and I responded, testily, too testily, "No, I didn't."

She stopped and looked at me inquisitively. "You didn't?" She was so pure—it slapped me in the face, and I recovered.

"Let me see it again," I said.

She jumped. I jumped. I saw it.

"You are right," I said. "It's jumping."

She smiled a brilliant smile of confidence.

Einstein said, "If you want your children to be brilliant, tell them fairy tales. If you want them to be very brilliant, tell them even more fairy tales."

I hope she always remembers that wondrous perspective and her magical ability to do amazing things. I know I will never forget, because for me, my magic fairy child will always move the moon.

SARAH JORDAN

HEALING WITH LOVE

Someone once asked me what was the worst thing I'd ever done, and I answered without hesitation: "I was so self-absorbed that I didn't nurture Rich enough when he was a baby." Rich is the second of my four children, born when I was nineteen years old. I certainly cared for him in all the physical ways a mother cares for her child. I fed him properly, changed his diapers, kept him clean, and ensured that he got the proper amount of sleep.

Still, if you're a parent, you know that's not enough. Usually, the intimacy is almost palpable when you watch a new mother and her infant gazing at each other. I loved my son, but our relationship lacked that bursting abundance of feeling. That sense of rapture, the connection, was missing. Frightened that I would never be able to live my own dream and become a teacher, I had turned myself off. I felt dead inside. I attended to Rich's needs meticulously, but in many ways I was simply going through the motions of motherhood.

At the age of six months, Rich developed a condition in which his body could not retain any nourishment. He ran very high fevers doctors could not control. No matter what we did, Rich continued to lose weight.

The time came when the doctor told me my baby was not likely to survive the night. In the early hours of the morning, I was sitting in a hospital room adjacent to where Rich struggled for life, tubes protruding from his tiny arms. An attending physician explained the severity of Rich's condition, trying to prepare me for the worst. Suddenly I realized I was watching our conversation from the other side of the room. What I had come to identify as "me," my everyday consciousness, was hovering in an upper corner, observing this sterile white room and the people in it in a way that was curiously unattached yet compassionate. I had read about out-of-body experiences but shrugged off those stories. Now I could clearly see the doctor speaking with a young, frightened mother: me.

At the same moment, I could sense my consciousness hovering in Rich's room. Gazing down at my baby, I was overcome with the realization that he was not starving for physical nourishment; rather, he needed the sustenance of the unconditional love I had denied him. His body hungered in that absence, unable to thrive.

In a flash, I found my consciousness back in my body, and I thanked the doctor for his words of condolence. Immediately I headed for Rich's room. Every sense in my body felt keenly aware and awake. As I approached the crib where he lay, my energy seemed to grow and expand to surround my ailing baby son. Suddenly I felt as if I were once again pregnant with my child. I completely enfolded Rich with my love, my being. Careful not to disturb the tubes, I reached into the crib and began stroking his face, reassuring my baby that I would never again deprive him of the love he needed. My heart opened completely. I connected with how much I loved him and wanted him in my life. I matured a great deal in those few minutes. For the remainder of the night, I sat next to Rich's crib, praying and feeling his soft skin against my hand.

Rich survived the night, and slowly the symptoms of his illness subsided. But doctors warned us about permanent neurological damage. When he was one year old, Rich still could not pull himself up. His arms and legs had little strength. In the weeks and months that followed, my husband, our parents, and I concentrated on nothing but pouring love into him. He grew stronger but didn't recover fully until he was almost three.

Years later, as I watched him play football in high school, I could hardly believe that as an infant this vital young athlete had been barely able to move his limbs. We each had experienced our own miracle. His was the miracle of physical healing. Mine was the miracle of moving past fear and doubt into a realm where I was free to love my son.

Rev. Mary Manin Morrissey

THE MIRACLE OF SELF-LOVE

Most of my life, I felt my dreams have been just out of reach. It seemed it took so much work to accomplish goals, and I was often left yearning for love or success. I was caught in a trap of working and getting nowhere. When my world appeared to be in complete disorder and I felt the depths of despair, I had been advised over and over again: *Love yourself.*

"How," I would ask, "do I love myself?" I didn't know. To me, loving yourself meant ending the pain with a new outfit or a hot fudge sundae. My mentors and counselors would quickly point out that such a remedy would last only as long as the experience of it lasted. I needed concrete steps to solve my dilemma, not vague advice.

Earning my bachelor's degree while working full time; raising my sons; getting divorced; and having major surgery weren't easy. But they were way stations toward my lifelong dream of living in Seattle.

The first step to my dream was to have a public relations career. What I found in Seattle were few jobs and hundreds of applicants. I struggled for four years, taking jobs on the fringe of public relations. Often I worked a full day, then volunteered and freelanced so I could improve my résumé. It was like holding two full-time jobs. I was deep into struggle and felt self-contempt for my inability to create the job and lifestyle I had dreamed of all those years.

After four years of this vicious circle, I was laid off my permanent job, with no immediate opportunities in front of me. I was scared and worried, yet I continued my "doing," going through the motions of job hunting for months—but with no results. Out of sheer desperation, I felt I had to give up the dream that had kept me going through most of my life.

Wanting to run away to a place of power and beauty, where I wasn't faced with the pain, I took some time away at my cousin's cabin on the ocean.

A remarkable thing happened there. For three days I did nothing but enjoy the scenery, meditate, and read. While checking my phone messages on the fourth day, I heard a call from an association with which I had interviewed months earlier. It was an offer for a public relations position. I realized then that "giving up" the struggle, trusting the process to allow goodness into my life, was the way I had loved myself.

What success I had ever experienced during my life had come to me with a great deal of struggle. This was the first demonstration that consciously letting go and trusting the outcome achieved something I longed for.

After two years, I was offered a wonderful job with the association's national headquarters, in Washington, D.C. It wasn't Seattle, but I didn't question the move, for I had learned that the best things in my life come to me without struggle or pain.

I would like to tell you that I have completely given up struggle, but I can't. Still, I have been blessed with patient friends, a loving family, and caring teachers, who listen to my frantic pleas when I forget I am the child of a loving Father.

I now believe "self-love" means going with ease and releasing the need to try and figure everything out by myself. I ask for help and then let go. I now regularly give God something to do.

JILL GOODWIN

III
FEEDING A WOMAN'S HEART

"Love is a fruit in season at all times and within reach of every hand."

—Mother Teresa

SNAPSHOTS OF THE HEART

The 1962 August moon gleamed across the white hood of the Ford Fairlane as Jason weaved his car between the huge moss-laden oaks lining my driveway. Shy and silent, I sat close to the passenger door, twisting a piece of my stiffly sprayed brown hair. The car rolled to a stop beneath the security lights that illuminated my home, and for a moment, Jason let the engine idle. With an inaudible sigh, I stole a last look at the Elvis-like lips that complemented his perfectly sculpted nose. The date I had dreamed about all through high school was ending on a "see you next lifetime" note.

Jason squeezed my hand at the door. "We'll do it again, Linda, sometime."

The words I wanted to say clung to my tongue like peanut butter, and instead of encouraging him to ask me out again, I smiled and said, "Thank you for a nice evening."

As we said good night, he squinted in the glare of the bright porch light, then looked at me with eyes that glistened like emeralds. Each of my senses recorded the moment like a snapshot: the sticky summer air touching our clasped hands, moonlight lunging between the tall pines in my yard, a cricket symphony strumming around us. Even his cologne mingled with the smell of the woods and found its way into that snapshot.

After he'd gone, I turned off the lights, while my heart sank like a rock in water. "I blew my chance with Jason!" I cried out, and stood in the dark, leaning against the partially opened front door. As I listened to the low rumble of his car in the distance, I knew my phone would gather a mountain of South Georgia dust before he called again. That night, I swallowed a large, unpalatable lump of rejection.

For days I wallowed in self-disgust over the romance that might have been had I not hidden my true personality under a facade called "the perfect date." If Jason had been unpopular or less intelligent or had a face like Quasimodo, I wouldn't have been afraid to show him the real Linda. But he had been captain of the football and basketball teams, class president, and a DJ at our small-town radio station. Aside from being impressed with his abilities and popularity, I was enamored of his good looks and intimidated by his intelligence.

Thoughts of college soon helped me bury my emotional snapshot of Jason, along with my feelings of rejection.

Twenty-three years later, I saw him at a class reunion.

"You look terrific!" Jason said, hugging me. I remarked about the George Hamilton splashes of gray at his temples. We talked casually, but it wasn't long before an undertow of old fears made me uneasy, and I put a crowd of schoolmates between us.

One spring day in 1996, after surviving most of the adult crises chronicled by Gail Sheehy in her book *Passages*, I answered the phone, surprised to hear a strong masculine voice. He spoke my name with such gusto, I thought I had won the *Reader's Digest* Sweepstakes.

"Linda! Do you know who this is?"

"No," I said, searching a mental file of men in my past.

"This is Jason."

After my initial shock, Jason and I began to piece together our school days. Like a couple of spirited five-year-olds, we plunged into our sandbox of memories and laughed at the many humorous things we did back then. We discussed our lives, faults, and failures with refreshing honesty and began to build a friendship based on truth.

Then out of the blue Jason asked a startling question.

"Linda, do you remember our date after graduation?"

"Well, I remember your old white Ford."

"What happened to us? How did you view that date?"

I laughed. "You rejected me! You never called again."

"No, Linda. I'll tell you what really happened. I was insecure," he admitted. "You were aloof, and I came from the poor side of town. I wasn't good enough for you. I was afraid to see you again. But I've thought about you all these years!"

With the honey of his truth, my thirty-four-year-old wall of rejection crumbled like old cookies at the bottom of the Oreo box. I saw the real Jason for the first time—a sensitive, down-to-earth man with a heart of love, a man with fears like me.

It's midsummer now, and I've replaced my old snapshot of Jason with new ones—like the one my senses take each evening when a golden streamer of sunlight stretches across the wide river to Jason and me on the grassy bank. Or the one that records the rhythmic lapping of water against the sailboat as we hang our feet off the floating dock and watch the mid-river porpoise ballet.

Best of all is the picture of tender hugs, rich laughter, and the growing love of two friends who found the courage to make snapshots of the heart together.

LINDA DUNIVIN

THE PAJAMA CONNection

People expected to hear I joined the Peace Corps to live a life of service, or to help those less fortunate, or at the very least because I'd lost my mind. The truth is I craved adventure, and for someone on a budget that couldn't even qualify as shoestring, it seemed the most convenient way. That is how, at twenty-two, I came to live on a Guatemalan mountaintop, in a mud hut eighteen kilometers from the closest road. The day I moved in, the welcoming committee consisted of one pit viper curled up under the wood-and-rope-frame bed, which I hacked to death with a machete. Shortly afterward, a neighbor stopped by to point out which of the insects inhabiting my adobe walls would "do nothing" and which would "kill you for certain." After the snake incident, the ritual of holding a candle to the wall each evening and squashing scorpions and tarantulas with a hiking boot before retiring to bed seemed like small beans. Under these circumstances, I readily jumped at the invitation to join a male Peace Corps friend on a trek to the ancient Guatemalan capital of Antigua to watch the Super Bowl in an American bar.

Dressed for the long hike and bus ride in 115-degree desert heat, I'd worn a long sheath dress, which hung limply off my body, and tied my red hair in a bun on the top of my head. By the time we reached our destination, sunburned and dirty, we were more than ready to simply sit back and vegetate in front of the TV. It was then that my companion chose to inform me how awful I looked. "On top of which," he said, "that dress looks like a nightgown. You look like you're wearing pajamas." Thinking his teasing was funny, he turned to the crowd of other Peace Corps Volunteers and Americans around us, urging, "Come on, don't you think she looks like she's wearing pajamas?" Slowly the man sitting in front of me turned around and looked me square in the eyes. "I think you look absolutely beautiful," he said, before turning his attention back to the game. I was smitten.

Back in my little hut the next day, I hatched The Plan. Asking around before I left the city, I had discovered that his name was Frank. A fellow Peace Corps Volunteer, he lived in a village ten hours away from mine. My mission was to arrange a chance meeting in the capital, where Volunteers converged the first weekend of each month to receive their monthly living stipend. That way he'd have the opportunity to ask me out—because, as all proper Catholic girls who attended the correct parochial schools learned early in life, a young lady never makes the first move, and she certainly never invites a man on a date. Problem was, the one time I did see him after that, he didn't ask me out, and then I didn't see him again for six months. And so I did what I wish they'd advocate more often in those proper parochial schools: I broke the rules.

I wrote Frank a letter, inviting him to meet me in the capital for dinner the night before the annual Fourth of July party at the American Embassy. I started out by reminding him who I was, and ended by telling him I would send him a telegram closer to the date, letting him know when and where to meet me. "If you're not interested," I concluded, "just don't show up, and I will never bother you again." I made each and every one of the men present in the Peace Corps office read my letter. "What do you think?" I asked. "I want to make sure it doesn't sound too forward or crass." It's perfect, was the resounding reply. "I've waited my whole life to get a letter like this," one dear friend said. "Don't change a thing." So I held my breath, slipped it into his mail slot there in the office, and returned home.

By noon the next day, I'd made the eighteen-kilometer hike up and then back down my mountain: Because of a series of bizarre and unfortunate incidents involving three rattlesnakes, a chicken, and a slab of marble, I found myself hitching a ride back to the embassy to fill out a crime report. Being so near the Peace Corps office for the second time in two days, I figured it made sense to swing by and check to see if Frank had dropped in and read his mail. I strolled through the back door and almost walked right into him, sitting on the edge of the sofa reading my letter. As I watched, he leaned forward, pen in hand, and began writing a note. Realizing he didn't know I stood behind him, I stole in a little closer to read over his shoulder. That way, if the news was bad, I could beat a hasty retreat back out the door without having to bear the humiliation of being turned down in person. "Dear Ellen," his letter began, "You could send me a telegram anytime, anywhere, and I would immediately come to be with you." Tap, tap, tap . . . I poked his shoulder and, to his startled look, smiled and said, "Here I am!"

We walked hand in hand to Burger King—quite the luxurious restaurant in those parts—to plan our first date, one month in the future. Having established the time and place of our next meeting, as well as our coinciding views on Eastern religions and Western politics, we walked to my bus station and he kissed me on the cheek before waving goodbye. When I finally did make it home late that day, I settled down by candlelight to write a letter to a friend back in the States. At the end I added a postscript: "I just made a date with the man I'm going to marry."

Our dinner date in the capital on July 4th turned into a week of breakfasts, lunches, and dinners. Three weeks later—one week before our next planned meeting—a haggard co-worker trekked up my mountain to bring me a telegram. "Let's never spend this much time apart again," it said. "Love, Frank." And we didn't, arranging to travel and work in each other's villages one week every month. On Christmas Eve, in an ancient monastery in the same little town where he first told me I was beautiful, he bent down on one knee and asked me to marry him.

As darkness fell on that magical night, we found a quiet restaurant where we could celebrate our good fortune with wine and cheese and roast lamb—so different from our usual fare of beans and eggs. Christmas being a family holiday in Central America, we were the only guests at the inn until halfway through the meal, when an elderly couple came in and took the table right next to ours. Curious, we thought, that they would sit so close when there were empty tables everywhere. But then our attention turned, and we ceased to notice them. Finished with our meal, we stood to head back out into the night, when the old woman reached out and touched my arm. "Excuse me," she said, as she grasped my hand. "I hate to intrude on such a special night, but I must ask you a question. The two of you look so happy: is this a special occasion?" Frank beamed as he replied, nodding toward me. "Yes, ma'am, it is. Tonight I asked her to become my wife." The old woman turned her gaze to the old man, and the two of them smiled deeply. Then the elderly gentleman looked first at me and then at my husband-to-be. "Fifty years ago tonight, I did the very same thing," he said to Frank. "Our wish for you on this Christmas Eve is that you will always be as happy as we have been."

We were married that spring in Virginia, surrounded by family and cherished friends. In addition to a gift, one woman brought a two-year-old letter with a postscript: "I just made a date with the man I'm going to marry."

Ellen Urbani Hiltebrand

> *"If we won't feel our emptiness,
> we won't find the depths of love available to us."*
> —Deborah Olive

PAIRS AND SPARES

As a never-married over-thirty woman, I didn't care for weddings. No, it was stronger than that. I *hated* weddings. I would sit in the pew, watching the church fill up like the loading of the ark, two by two, all the while moaning under my breath, "Where's *my* other giraffe?" The only thing that made this particular wedding bearable was the obvious love the bridal pair had for each other.

The bride and I shared the same first name, which meant that the whole time she was taking her vows, I mentally took them with her—you know, just in case I never got to actually say them myself, or as a means of practice if someday I did marry. When the ceremony concluded, I noticed a handsome, smiling man about two rows back, all by himself. No ring on his left hand. Hmm. I knew vaguely that he worked at the radio station with Doug, the groom. Determined to learn more, I headed in his direction, thinking: Well, I can at least say hello!

So I did. And he did. Nice smile, warm handshake. Then he asked me, "What is that sculpture up in front of the church?" The sculpture was a free-form artistic interpretation of a cross, not an unusual thing to have in a church. He may not know what a cross is, I thought. Hey, he may not know who God is! Maybe I ought to introduce the two of them. Off I went, describing the cross itself, repentance, baptism, Acts 2:38, regeneration, everything this guy needed to know.

I went on and on, as only I can, while he smiled and nodded and smiled and nodded. Hey, I've got a live one here! I thought to myself. Then, slowing down to catch my breath, I said, "So tell me a little about yourself."

"Well . . . ," he said slowly, "I'm an ordained minister."

I was speechless. (This is rare.) "A minister?" I finally said, as a smile slid up one side of his face. "No kidding!" I stammered. "Did I get everything right?"

"You did well," he assured me, and we both laughed.

One thing Bill found out about me right away was that I cared more about his relationship with God than any potential relationship with me. And that was exactly what attracted him to me. That and my level of self-acceptance. And my laugh!

We stood there and talked in the sanctuary until it was empty, and I realized I didn't have the faintest idea where the wedding reception was. Bill had saved the directions and said, "Why don't you follow me?"

Happy to.

At the reception, we kept an eye on each other as we mingled around the room, finally ending up at the same table. (Imagine that.) More talking, more sharing, then finally we exchanged business cards, and I said, "Call me sometime."

Now came the big wait. Four or five days later (not wanting to appear overanxious, he later said), Bill called. I wasn't home, but my answering machine was. I can still remember coming in and finding the usual "0" replaced with a "1." For a single woman who had not dated in years, any night without a "goose egg" on the machine was a good night!

The message was short and sweet. A warm voice with a Kentucky twang said, "I wondered if you might like to go to dinner with me sometime next week?" I might. "Please give me a call back, Liz," were his final words. Not wanting to appear overanxious, either, I waited four or five seconds before dialing his number.

Our first date came two weeks later; our wedding date was exactly eight months after that. (The only reason we waited that long is that it takes a while to special-order a custom-built size twenty wedding gown.) We'll be forever grateful to Liz and Doug for inviting both of us to their wedding, never dreaming that one ceremony would lead to another.

LIZ CURTIS HIGGS

THE LUCKY PHOTO

My dad was a sophomore at Texas A & I, taking twenty-two hours a semester and working his way through school with a job at a place called the Spudnut Shop. A spudnut is a doughnut, except that it's made with potato flour.

Dad had to be at work at three in the morning, to put fresh newspapers on the floor. The papers were supposed to catch the grease and flour. Dad was on his hands and knees that fall, spreading out pages from the *Kingsville Record*. One night his bleary eyes fell on a photo of a young woman who'd been named the local Farm Bureau beauty queen. To Dad, it was the face of an angel. He carefully ripped the picture out of the paper, folded it, and stuck it in his wallet.

Six months flew by. One April day, a fraternity brother asked my dad, "Hey, Darrell, you goin' to the big Lantana ball?"

It was the biggest social event of the school year. It was also costly for a young man struggling to pay tuition.

"Well," Darrell replied, pulling the photo out of his wallet, "if you can get me a date with this girl, I'll go."

"Epsie? Sure, I've known her all my life. You've got a deal, pal."

The day of the ball was rainy. Darrell, in his haste between classes and work, dropped his billfold in a puddle. The picture of Epsie was ruined. He was sad, but then he remembered he'd see the real young lady behind the smile in just a few hours.

The "blind date" (at least it was a blind date for Epsie) was like the stuff you hear about in fairy tales. They danced all night. Darrell thought Epsie was even prettier than her picture. Epsie was still in high school, and she had to be home at midnight. After walking her to her front porch, Darrell kissed her on the forehead and told her he'd call her soon. He didn't tell her right then, but the moment Epsie smiled at him that night, she went from a picture in his wallet to a place in his heart.

Fourteen months later, when Darrell and Epsie became engaged, the newspaper ran the same photo Darrell had torn out the year before, because it was his favorite.

They married in July on Friday the thirteenth, over objections that they were too young and from different religions and that to wed on such a date was unlucky.

The Spudnut Shop no longer exists, but my parents' union is still standing, more than forty years later. I wish I could tell you I look like my beauty queen mother. However, the legacy of love I've inherited is much more important.

Any Friday the 13th is now celebrated in my family, no matter what month it falls in . . . and my dad still carries a yellowed clipping of a girl with big dimples and the eyes of an angel. Dad says Mom is all the luck he's ever needed.

LORRI VAUGHTER ALLEN

"Whoever lives true life will love true love."
—ELIZABETH BARRETT BROWNING

MERCY STREET

I looked down at the all too familiar handwriting and saw the ink beginning to run, a river of tears and snow. Stillness surrounded me, an endless silence as large, heavy snowflakes continued to drift downward from a wintry New York City sky.

My heart ached with love, with longing, and I thought back to his first letter, the one detailing his arrival in Nicaragua and his forever optimistic nature.

My dearest. They always began the same. *My dearest. I miss you terribly and hope all is well. I have been made to feel very welcome. My "practice" consists of a room about six feet by eight, with a bed and a wooden table and two chairs. Sadly, there is no shortage of patients but all the more reason I'm glad I came. There is one other doctor here, Enrique. He is very skilled and, of even more importance, can make sense of my appalling Spanish! I have been telling him all about you. I can't wait to see you again. Love and kisses, Steven.*

Steven and I met in South Africa. I was there making a documentary on apartheid, and he, fresh out of residency, was volunteering with a group called Doctors Without Borders. I liked him the moment we met. He was tall and lean, and he radiated a calm and unpretentious spirit. I liked his smile too. It came easily and would light up his often troubled eyes, if only for a moment. I used to watch him at the makeshift clinic they had set up in Soweto. He was always there, with a consistency that came straight from the heart. He trusted and believed in people, but most of all, he hoped for them.

It was on a Tuesday that he asked if he could accompany me out to one of the homelands, where I had finally been given permission to film. I agreed, and the next twenty-four hours, shared atop an open truck, bouncing along rough terrain, sealed our friendship. I have often thought of our first meeting and have come to believe that there are some people in this world whom we have an unspoken connection to, in a way that defies explanation.

We continued to write to each other when he returned to New York and I went on to South America, to collect stories on *los desaparecidos,* the "disappeared ones." I found myself waiting for his letters with a gothic anxiety. They were long and intimate, like an ongoing conversation, and through our words we came to know each other and, I suspect, ourselves. When I finally returned to New York, the first thing I did was go to see Steven at the hospital where he worked.

I will never forget the look on his face when a colleague of his tapped him on the shoulder and he turned around to see me standing there. I wish I could capture and bottle that moment like a perfume. He came straight over to me, and without saying a word, put his arms around me and gave me the longest and sweetest kiss of my life. Although I never doubted the sincerity of his letters, with that kiss I knew we belonged to each other.

We went out for dinner to a small café that featured home cooking and was frequented by students who missed Mom's meat loaf. I felt an overwhelming happiness that night, the kind you feel when in the company of good friends.

I think one of the things I loved most about Steven was that he preferred conversation to television. He told me that we would be good together because doctors can heal the body, but artists, they heal the soul. I had never thought of myself as an artist, I was just someone who loved making films, the way he loved being a doctor.

We got an apartment together on Mercy Street. He liked the

name and felt it boded well for our future, believing that I would have to have a forgiving nature to put up with his hours, and he as well to accept my "artistic temperament." Not that he ever complained I was moody, "just a million miles away, someplace I can't go." It was prior to our second Christmas that he made his decision to go to work in a remote village in Nicaragua.

We were walking down the hospital corridor, with its pale-green walls decorated with bits of tinsel and drawings the children had done.

I asked him why he wanted to go.

"For the money," he quipped.

"Right," I said. The job paid sixteen dollars a month. "I thought you were happy here."

"When I leave here, there'll be someone to take my place. Besides, you always tell me that if you can help, you should. Remember?"

He had me there, and I reminded myself that he had never once put up an objection when I was off and running on some project, despite the worry it caused him. So I simply asked, "When do you leave?"

"In February."

"Well," I said, "I guess we better start on your Spanish lessons."

"Kiss me," he said.

"*Bésame*," I corrected, and kissed him.

We resumed our letter writing.

My dearest. At last I have made a favorable impression on everyone, though not by my medical skill, but rather by restoring a generator with the help of another "medico"—that is what they call us. There was much celebration when several of the houses lit up. The people here are very gentle, shy almost, and it is hard to comprehend how anyone would wish to harm them. I shall be expecting full details of your visit in the next letter. All my love, Steven.

My trip to Nicaragua came eight months later, after a letter from Enrique, telling me that there had been a raid on the village and how many had been killed, including Steven. He had been out in the field, attending a wounded child, when he was shot.

I stood in the silence of the snow and slowly opened the letter Steven had left for me "just in case."

My dearest, for dearest you will always be. I can say of my life that I am resting close to the people I came to help and to love. In a place where I expected to find only sorrow, they brought me friendship and joy. Keep on walking, my love, and know that I am always with you. Steven.

He had enclosed a black-and-white photograph of himself and Enrique, standing in front of their office. He looked a little thinner but in a strong, wiry sort of way, and his hair had grown and was combed back. He looked contented, fulfilled.

I turned the photograph over and read what he had written. *Homo sum: Humani nihil a me alienum puto.* "I am a man: I count nothing human of indifference to me." I sat down on a damp stone bench, and I wept.

Sometimes when I am walking down a familiar haunt of ours in New York, something will trigger a memory of him, so vivid, so sharp it leaves me breathless. I used to think that maybe it wasn't good to love someone so much. That the idea of losing the loved one would be too great to bear. Now I know differently.

A friend said to me, "He was a hero," and I smiled to myself, thinking what he would have thought of that. He was not a hero. Steven was an ordinary man with extraordinary ideas. From him I derived strength and courage. I knew about the frailty of the human soul, but he taught me that the miracle of the human spirit is to give.

HOLLY FITZHARDINGE

> *"Whatever you do to find a relationship,*
> *you must continue doing to keep a relationship."*
> —Susan Bradley

LOVE IS NOT FOR THE FAINT OF HEART

A walk on a beautiful September night shouldn't have meant an ending. The moon had been full, leaves crunching beneath our feet. The air was crisp and clear. Like us, a neighbor's cat was taking his usual evening stroll, and Mrs. Myrtle had given a friendly wave as she took out her trash.

Now, home alone, I wandered around my apartment, remembering the places that once held his things. The cup on the sink in the bathroom, which used to hold two toothbrushes, now held one. The shaving cream and razor were gone. The chocolate ice cream, still in the freezer, was his favorite. The bed was made with military purpose and hospital corners. The neatness of every room marked his effort.

I opened the closet, knowing I had overlooked nothing when I helped him pack. I searched the floor for a stray tie or sneaker. How I wished that I had not been so thorough. I looked at the empty section of closet space, missing his freshly starched shirts. I stared at the landing, looking hard for his shoes. The tears blurred my eyes, and I wondered if the ache would ever end. I remembered the whole night: it played continuously in my head.

"I don't know what to do," he'd said, with tears in his eyes. The pain seeped into every action and word.

"I love you enough to let you go," I said. My heart ached

with the thought of losing him. We had worked so hard to keep each other. But our families didn't seem to understand our closeness; instead they were deeply upset about our sixteen-year year age difference.

"I can't do it. I can't leave you. We have so many dreams," he responded.

I thought of a few, including buying a house together and finishing my education. We had spent many nights discussing all our dreams until dawn. We shared a deepening love and a growing spirituality. I thought of our dog and cat, each of which had lost a caring friend.

We held each other, knowing that we had fought so long and it was over. The dreams were meant to stay just that, dreams. The tears soaked our faces and clothes. I shuddered with sobs. I did not want to cry. I did not want to make this decision any harder for him. I loved him too much. I never wanted to cause him any pain.

"I'll help you pack. Come on—if we're going to do this, we have to do it now or I won't be able to let you leave."

I got up from the couch and started to gather his toothbrush, comb, and blow dryer from the bathroom, shirts, pants, and ties from the closet, sweats, bathrobe, and other assorted clothes from the bedroom. I swiped at the tears on my face as I packed his things. He just stood there dumbfounded. I had to make him go. It was best for him, for us. I never wanted him to feel as if I had held him back. I couldn't let him regret his decision if he stayed.

I helped him load everything in the car. We shut the door—the perfect punctuation mark for that whole evening.

We caught each other's hands, and we walked away from the car. We held hands and talked softly. It was very late. I couldn't remember the words we spoke. I could only remember his thumb caressing my hand. My eyes blurred as we walked. I wanted to huddle closer to him, but that would only make it harder. Finally, almost by accident, we reached his car again.

We wrapped our arms around each other, holding on frantically.

"I'm so sorry," he choked out.

"I know."

He got in the car and drove away. I stood on the porch, watching his taillights disappear. I stayed there a very long time. I sank to the steps and willed that he turn around and make everything all right. I prayed for him to come home. I needed him.

I had done what was right, yet the pain was extreme. I cried and cried till my head pounded and my eyes burned.

In the days that followed, I would jump at the ringing of the phone or the doorbell. I was so lost. I ached for his arms. I cried constantly, and I thought I saw him everywhere. I took two personal days and stayed in bed. I finished all the chocolate ice cream as I watched a sappy movie that only made me cry harder.

I stayed in the bathtub for hours. I'd let the water get cold and then just refill the tub. Sometimes I didn't realize it had gone cold till I was shaking with chills.

I walked the path that we had walked every day. I didn't talk to anyone about the pain. It was my own. It was all I had left of him, and I didn't want to share that.

Late one Monday night, the doorbell rang. After two weeks, I still jumped at the sound of a ringing phone or a visitor at the door, not knowing, but always hoping, it was him. I put on my old flannel bathrobe and went down the stairs, turning on lights as I went. I opened the door a little and peered out. On the front porch was my sweet honey.

I stood there for a long time, then I pushed the door open and wrapped my arms tightly around him. I cried. He cried.

"I couldn't do it," he said.

"I couldn't, either." I was crying and laughing at the same time.

CHASSIDY A. F. PERSONS

MARRIAGE ENCOUNTER

My sister Bonnie was ecstatic over the new man in her life, convinced he was "the one." Ernie was ruggedly handsome, easy to be with, caring and sensitive, and he made her laugh. And before he even kissed her for the very first time, he told her that he was the kind of guy who dated only one woman at a time. On their fourth date he told Bonnie he would marry her.

So when it happened that a significant amount of time passed with no marriage proposal, Bonnie began to nudge him toward the idea of a bigger commitment. However, with the uneventful passing of their second Valentine's Day together, she decided it was time—time to strengthen her resolve. Bonnie drove over to his place, all the while rehearsing just what she wanted to say to him. She knew she must strike during the time his attention was exclusively hers—before the Bull's game began, during the short commercial breaks, or at halftime. "Brief but to the point," she told herself again. As she entered his condo, Bonnie told him straight out, "Ernie Krause, we need to talk!" Surprising her, he immediately flopped himself down upon his threadbare couch—his bachelor throne. But before she could utter even one of the words she had rehearsed, he asked, "Honey, before you start, would you grab me one of those mints out of that box in the fridge, since you're already up and all."

Bonnie wondered aloud if this man had any limits to his audacity. He just laughed his little dry laugh while she stomped off to the kitchen like an angry, yet obedient, child. She thought her tone had conveyed her urgency in discussing her feelings with him. How, then, had she ended up playing golden retriever, loyally fetching a mint for her bachelor king?

These were no ordinary cheap mints. They were his Marshall Field favorites, which Bonnie had given him on Valentine's Day, a few days before. The same Valentine's Day he showed up forty-five minutes late for their date, the same Valentine's Day he gave her a silly card. And now this!

She recalled the weak explanation he managed to offer for his being so late. Something about having to take care of a matter he could no longer neglect. Bonnie wondered what could be more important than showing up on time for a Valentine date with the girl he'd been claiming to love for the past year and a half.

By the time she reached the refrigerator, anger got the best of her. Bonnie opened the door with such a vengeance that condiments crashed to the floor. She thought about just leaving them where they had come to rest. On second thought, she said to herself, "OK. One of us has to be the adult in this relationship." She returned the jars to their place on the door, then found his prized box of mints on the top shelf of his otherwise almost barren refrigerator. She flipped off the top of the box, to reveal a bold message: It read, very simply: *Bonnie, will you marry me?* Below these words was yet another surprise. There, within the center of a red heart, he had carefully tied the most beautiful engagement ring she had ever seen. Her rage suddenly turned to joy, as tears flooded his kitchen floor!

CHRISTINE D. MAREK

IV
MAXIMUM EXPOSURE

*"At times, all we have to do in life is show up,
be present,
and allow the magic to unfold."*

—Yitta Halberstam and Judith Leventhal

"As a dreamer you will be laughed at. . . . Thank them!"
—Author unknown

SOAP BOX DERBY

It was 1972, the year of Watergate, of Shirley Chisholm's presidential candidacy, of the hits "I Am Woman" and "One Tin Soldier." And it was the first year girls were allowed to race in the Fargo Soap Box Derby.

Good thing, too. My family was in the throes of race fever. My brother had won the local derby the previous summer. Winners cannot compete again.

"Hey, it's my turn! I can do this!" I announced.

And Dad said, "Of course you can."

Was I a women's libber? A tomboy?

No. I was thirteen and had no need of these labels. I learned embroidery and motorcycling with equal attention. My family did not draw such demarcations.

But that summer I would learn all about them.

My first clue should have been that none of my girlfriends spent their evenings in a low-ceilinged basement, pondering wind resistance and wheel-bearing lubricants. Building my car took a year of evenings and weekends. A year of missed TV and teen hangouts. A year of fiberglass shards in my arms and sanding dust in my mouth.

But there was another taste in my mouth—the taste of victory.

And of course I would win. Hadn't my brother won? Wasn't my dad the best car designer there ever was, the best teacher of craftsmanship? Wasn't my mom wonderfully supportive, doing dishes my nights so I could descend the stairs with Dad?

Oh, I didn't always want to descend those stairs. I can still see Dad's face, set firm in answer to my adolescent whines. But the cardinal rule of the Soap Box Derby is that a race car has to be made entirely by its driver's hands.

In early summer, my car came out of the dim basement and into the sunlit backyard. And what a car! All sleek and streamlined, all black and shiny with my name in red letters. I knew every inch of that car. That car and I would cross the finish line together.

July 8: Race Day! There was a parade and celebrities and hullabaloo, but I was in a bubble of calm certainty. Even in the face of the fact there were seventy other challenging racers—five of them girls!

The heats began. My car was fast, and I drove straight. I was winning each race.

Then the trouble began.

And there's always a troublemaker. One of the racers started to taunt me, sitting prominently near the starting gate and shouting, "Cheater! You didn't build that car!"

I ignored him for one race, but after several more he was getting under my skin. Why was he doing this? What had I done?

The field was being narrowed, as the heats eliminated racer after racer. I raced that taunting boy and won, which felt good and right. I thought that would end my troubles.

Little did I know. He was just the herald, the harbinger of the hue and cry to come.

Ah, but the final finish line flashed under me, and I knew I had won. As I had known all along I'd win. I clambered out of my car, and crazy images appeared and disappeared in split seconds, like a frantic dream: race officials grabbing at me, a TV camera zooming in, a woman talking excitedly into a microphone.

And above all, Dad's exultant face. "You did it! You did it, Marci!"

But the frenzy of the win soon turned into a furor of controversy. I can still see the apoplectic faces of several of the losing boys' fathers. Accusations flew, terrible and unfounded, as they tried to block me (the girl) from going to the next step, the international race in Akron, Ohio.

"She didn't build that car."

"No way she did. Her father's an architect," the last word spat as if it were an obscenity.

"A cheater shouldn't represent our city at the international race."

The media got wind of the fracas. I was on TV. I was interviewed by the newspapers. Radio call-in shows buzzed with callers, both defiling and defending.

Eventually, I sorted it out within myself. I knew I hadn't cheated. I knew they were just sore losers. I knew they would have been sore losers even if a boy had won. But it was plain my being a girl added to their anger.

So I learned that it did matter that I was a girl in a boys' world. And then, standing straight and silent, I unlearned it. Because what did it really matter?

I went to the international race, because I belonged there with the two hundred sixty other contestants from all around the globe who had built cars, raced—and won.

MARCI MADSEN FULLER

THE MIRACLE BUS

It was a freezing December night. Exhausted from an intense day of work and the holiday frenzy, I stood at my usual bus stop, on Broadway and Ninth Street in Greenwich Village. Since I hadn't had a spare second to chow down, I was stressed to the max, and my blood sugar level was dropping rapidly. Huddling beneath Woolworth's faceless windows, appreciative of the shelter their awnings provided from the whipping wind, I wondered why every other bus but mine seemed to roll by.

I yearned to go home, curl up under my covers, destress, veg out, but I was on my way to see a new printer, having procrastinated until the final moments before my photography exhibition. I was musing on all this when my bus—the M6—finally pulled in.

"Do you go straight down Broadway, below Canal?" I queried. Last night the bus had randomly decided to turn. So much for the consistency of Manhattan mass transit!

The bus driver, a big black man, smiled reassuringly.

Token in slot, I collapsed into the first single seat—designed for one passenger only, it is the favorite of lone New Yorkers. Across the aisle, two men were seated together, the bus's only passengers besides myself. The first, a tall, lanky African-American, holding a large book, *The Now Bible*, greeted me with a warm "Good evening!" The second man, a dark, mustached Latino, winked a welcome.

I giggled!

Then, without pause, the men and the driver broke into a gleeful, foot-stompin' gospel tune.

"Do you sing together in a choir?" I managed to interject.

"Oh, no, we just met!"

Soon sounds praising the Lord, singing of angels and "The

Good World a-Comin' " reverberated throughout the bus. I found myself tapping my feet, swaying to the beat, and humming along.

Miraculously, the bus never stopped to pick up any other passengers, and I was the grateful recipient of a spontaneous private concert.

I was so blissed out, I missed my stop and had to walk back several blocks.

But when I emerged from that bus, smiling, I was relaxed, peaceful, and ready to embrace the world.

"Thank you, thank you, thank you!" I called as I got off.

Just think, if all the buses in New York City were filled with song, what a different place it would be!

JILL LYNNE

THE POWER OF LOVE

When I turned twenty-four, I thought the world was my oyster. I had a wonderful job with lots of growth opportunity, I had good friends and family nearby, and I had an affordable, brand-new apartment two miles from the beach in Fort Lauderdale. I was perfectly content with my life the way it was.

I have always been a creature of routine. In my early twenties, I knew that I wanted to work slowly toward my Ph.D. and focus on my career. Marriage and family were not even a part of my grand design. Always wanting to be in control of everything, including my emotions, I never mapped out for myself the undeniable power of true love.

The weekend after my twenty-fourth birthday, I went out with my girlfriend Mara. She insisted on taking me to the latest club in Boca Raton, aptly named Heaven. Anyone who is single and living in the South Florida area can tell you how old the club scene becomes once you're past the age of twenty-two. I was sick of flirting with tourists from other places who were only out to "score" with a Florida girl. One-night stands were not my thing. I really didn't want to go to a club; but after much arm twisting from Mara, I finally went.

I remember standing in the club with my friend, my arms folded across my chest. I had a scowl on my face that would've intimidated most any person, and yet there came Andrew, walking toward me. I wonder even today what could have been remotely inviting about me! Nevertheless, he introduced himself, and Andrew and I talked and danced all night. He was everything I was *not* looking for: a tourist from New York who was in Florida visiting his grandmother. I felt I was wasting my time even chatting with this guy. But maybe it was a look he gave me, or the way he laughed. Whatever "it" was, it was starting to happen. I'd never given my number to a guy in a bar before. On this night, I made an exception.

Andrew snuck in a quick kiss as the valet brought our cars around to the front of the club. I expected never to hear from him again; but he began calling at eight A.M. the next morning. Over the course of the day, he invited me to go to the beach and finally to dinner with his entire family. I declined, unable to see getting past the introductions: "Mom, this is Michelle. I picked her up in a bar last night. . . ." We finally agreed to meet again, just the two of us. I couldn't believe myself as I gave what amounted to a total stranger my address and directions to my apartment. All those seminars and workshops I had attended in my college days about how to protect yourself from dangerous situations, and here I was with a neon sign, inviting danger into my home.

I felt breathless when I saw Andrew standing at my door in a suit (I have a weakness for suits!). He had sparkling blue eyes and a generous, loving smile.

At a waterside restaurant, we giggled about meeting in Heaven, and we laughed even harder at the fact that I had been a strict vegetarian for ten years and he was in the wholesale meat business. What a pair we made! There was no topic we couldn't discuss, it seemed, and we felt we had known each other for a lifetime. What clinched it for me was when he asked permission to kiss me good night. I remember saying something like "What took you so long," and as he kissed me, I felt my knees weaken and my heart begin to race. He was different in some inexplicable but wonderful new way.

We went out every night that Andrew was in Florida, and he called me the night he went home to New York. After talking nightly on the phone for several weeks, I went to New York to see him. I wanted to know if there was really anything more than an initial attraction between us. He was so nervous when he picked me up at the airport that we kept getting lost as he attempted to drive us back to his apartment. At the end of the weekend, when we were confirming my flight home with my mother over the phone, Andrew asked me, "Does your mom know I love her daughter?" I didn't "say it back" until two weeks later, when I flew up to attend a wedding with him.

For six months we survived endless plane trips, outrageous phone bills, and frustrations with loneliness and unsupportive friends. We endured chicken pox (he gave them to me, so we had to go through them twelve hundred miles apart!) and self-doubts. But through it all, a powerful love was blossoming between us, distance and all.

Somehow, looking back, I had to have been so totally in love that rational thought was no longer part of my state of mind. Where was my head, to go and quit my great job, give up my free graduate school opportunities, leave my friends, my family, my secure lifestyle, and move to New York to live with a man I had seen only a few days a month for less than a year? And so, with all rational sense tossed aside, I packed up and moved. No friends, no job, just love in my heart. Looking back, we were nuts!

Shortly after I'd made New York my new home, we were driving over the George Washington Bridge. Andrew asked, "Michelle, will you please marry me? I want to spend the rest of my life with my best friend. I love you." Through tears, I said "yes" a hundred times over.

Our honeymoon has never ended. We've built a life together, bought a home, had a child, with another on the way. We always talk about our future. We have discovered that, as much as we have in common, there are many things we feel differently about. But it's those differences that make us fall in love with each other again and again each day.

Now I'm thirty, and as I look back (and ahead), I can say without a doubt that love is a powerful thing. It binds unlikely people together and helps them discover qualities within themselves and others that they never knew they had. To think that I expected to plan out every step of my life! To think that I believed there were no such things as soul mates and deep, passionate love. How was it that I had become so set in my ways at such a young age, determined to live my life according to a self-imposed code that left no room for chance, for magic, for the unpredictable power of love?

How lucky for me that I was given an opportunity to follow either my head or my heart. Thank goodness I went to a higher authority and stepped into Heaven one night for a visit. I pray I never have to leave.

Michelle Cohen

THE VIRTUES OF MR. WRONG!

For most women, there's an unspoken rule that one of our life's missions is to find and capture our "knight in shining armor"—to be diligent and deliberate in our efforts and, once successful, to buy into the American Dream of a home with white picket fence, a family, and, of course, "happily ever after."

It took many years of trial and error in my eternal search for Mr. Right before I would come to discover that there is much to be said for Mr. Wrong too.

Mr. Wrong, for the record, is not someone who is otherwise spoken for—that would be Mr. Stupid.

Mr. Wrong is not a man who is physically or emotionally abusive to women in order to prove his so-called manhood—that would be Mr. On Your Way Out the Door.

Mr. Wrong is not someone doing time behind bars or living the type of lifestyle that would indicate he will be one day—that would be Mr. Some Folks Are Best Left Alone.

But not all Mr. Wrongs are wrong. In your search for your life partner, don't overlook men who could provide moral support, quality time, fun and laughter, and invaluable life experiences. I call men like that Mr. Right for Now.

One of my Mr. Wrongs was handsome, six feet two, intelligent, affectionate, articulate, humorous, and exciting. We met at work. He was clearly not marriage material. And I knew it. He was deemed Mr. Wrong for matrimonial purposes because we were extreme opposites and at different stages in life. I am shy, serious, and ambitious by nature. He is a "people" person, spontaneous and laid back, who takes very little seriously. I'm Catholic, he is nondenominational. I'm into Barry Manilow and Johnny Mathis. He enjoys disco and rap. Not to mention the age difference. But when we came together, he became Mr. Right for Now, and there was not a better time to be had. He taught me to live for today, to plan less, to experience more, and to find something worthy of laughter each day. I taught him the importance of honesty and compassion and the beauty of simple pleasures—like quiet evenings at home.

Years ago, I would not have wasted my time with a man so different from me. I was on a mission back then, consumed with a mental checklist of what Mr. Right would say and do in order to qualify as "the one." Every potential suitor would be scrutinized according to these standards, and the ones who failed the initial screening would be ousted early in the game. But that was yesterday.

Now I know that if we are receptive students, life teaches us very valuable life lessons when it comes to matters of the heart. An incurable romantic by nature, I'm no longer looking for Mr. Right, though I haven't given up hope that he exists and that one day he'll find me! Until that day, I've discovered the temporary but ever-sweet joy derived from experiencing some of life's journey with Mr. Wrong.

JENNIFER BROWN BANKS

*"Imagine the best day of your life.
Now imagine living that way 365 days a year."*
—Author unknown

GINNY'S EXCELLENT ADVENTURE

Ginny was a faithful wife for forty-two years when her husband, Norman, died of cancer. She had spent two years nursing him through his illness. Throughout his career, Norman worked for the railroad, so the last thing he wanted to do when he wasn't working was travel. Ginny, on the other hand, had an unfulfilled passion for travel. They did drive to Florida once, but as soon as they got there Norman wanted to drive home. To hear Ginny tell it, she barely had time to use a Florida rest room.

After his death, with no one to care for at home, Ginny declared, "I'm hittin' the road." And hit the road she did. Using her retirement money, she traveled to the Galápagos Islands, Africa, China, South America, Fiji, England, Australia, and New Zealand. "Not too bad for an ol' gal who has barely ever been out of St. Louis," Ginny used to say.

When Ginny's son invited her to join him, his wife, and their friends on an eight-day rafting trip down the Grand Canyon, her response was predictable: "Let's go!" Never mind that she had never been rafting and couldn't even swim.

It was on that rafting trip that I met Ginny: a vivacious seventy-year-old who held on to the ropes till her knuckles were white and laughed the entire way at the sheer thrill of living.

The Canyon is a spiritual place, and for eight days the only song I could remember was the first verse of "Amazing Grace." Ginny didn't mind. She'd ask me to sing it over and over. Once back home, she mailed me the words to verses two through six: "Just for a change," she said.

Two years later, Ginny got a stomachache. She thought it was just too much travel food. By the time she got around to seeing a doctor between trips, he said there was no point in operating. She had six months to live.

"Mom, what do you want to do with your remaining time?" asked her son. "I want to travel, silly, just as long as I can. And I want to go to Paris."

They came to visit us in North Carolina for Thanksgiving, and we all danced the macarena in the living room. They went to a Texas beach for the warmth, but they never made it to Paris. Ginny knew she was winding down and wanted to go home to St. Louis, back to the house she and Norman had shared.

On my way to Chicago to give a talk, I had a premonition that I needed to stop off in St. Louis to visit Ginny. I called her son to ask if I could come the next day. His reply left me chilled to the bone. "You'd better hurry. Mom just announced she has picked tomorrow to die." The next day was April 15, and Ginny liked the thought of "going out" on the day taxes were due.

I put on my angel earrings for the trip. gold hoops with angels sitting inside, swinging on my shoulders. I wanted all the angels I could gather with me for this journey.

During the flight, I realized that one of my angel earrings was missing. The flight attendants and I practically ripped the airplane seat apart, but one angel earring had simply vanished. As I took off my lone earring, I couldn't understand why this was happening. Even if it was only symbolic, it felt like my angels had deserted me.

By the time I arrived in St. Louis, Ginny was alert but weak. The hospice nurse came, and we gave Ginny a bath, changed her sheets, and clothed her in new pajamas. As I held her fragile body in my arms, I realized we were preparing her for her shroud. But Ginny was not sad. She made her last day an event.

Laughing and teasing about her lime-green sheets, she told me, "Citrus is the hottest fashion color, and I intend to leave in style."

After the nurse left, Ginny asked me to sing to her. I held her close to me once again and sang the only verse I could remember of "Amazing Grace." Her last words to me were, "Now you go to Chicago and give a *really* good speech!" It suddenly struck me that when I'm old and I look back on my life, I don't want any regrets. I want to have packed as much into life as Ginny did in her last years.

When I left her room, her daughter handed me a small box. "Several days ago, even before she knew you were coming, Mom said she wanted you to have these."

Inside the box was a pair of her favorite gold hoop earrings. I understood immediately why my earring had disappeared. Ginny is now the angel swinging from those gold hoops. She is constantly reminding me to live life as she did—to the fullest. Together we're having one excellent adventure!

BAILEY ALLARD

MY TRUCKER

The wind roared all night, and the rain fell hard. Quietly I leaned over Joshua, stared at his face, and knew he was sleeping peacefully. As I slyly took one giant step over him, onto the front seat, I felt his hand grab my ankle, and I could feel the smile spread across my face.

"How'd you know I made a movement?" I asked. "I was so quiet."

He responded with a grin. "You can't sneak out! I know every motion of this truck, and you know by now you can't put anything over on me."

I'd been so sure he was sound asleep! Six weeks on the road, and it was Thanksgiving morning. We were on the last leg of our cross-country trip in Joshua's eighteen-wheeler moving van, on our way to Florida from Texas. The schedule was to unload in northern Florida and drive to the south and stay in a condo on the beach for a few days of relaxation. Then he would be off west again, and I would fly back to New York. This spur-of-the-moment trip for me—a fifty-year-old grandmother and "prima donna"—had been wonderful, and I was going to miss him.

But today I missed home. Living in a truck, not being able to jog my familiar road every morning, contact with only one person—it was all beginning to get to me. One part of me loved being alone with my trucker, but something in me was off today.

As we traveled down the highway, I listened to the soft swish of the windshield wipers. I thought of Mom. She was probably making her homemade cranberry sauce right now, then she'd start her special pumpkin pie with heavy cream and brandy, to take to my sister's house this afternoon. My sister Kathy would be setting the table with beautiful family china about now, for our traditional Thanksgiving. I should be in my kitchen, making corn pudding and the cream cheese brownies everyone said were a "must." Of course, my father would stop by. He always drove around the morning of the holiday, stopping in to see each of his three daughters. Daydreaming, I could actually hear his car pulling into the driveway and coming to a halt—when I realized we had actually stopped! Josh had pulled up to a service station. I ran to the pay phone and called my oldest sister.

"Happy Thanksgiving!" I said, about to cry.

"Hi!" Barb answered. "You know, I keep thinking it's so cool and exciting you're on the road. Its not like hopping on a plane and missing everything along the way. Not too much going on here—we're just doing the same old Thanksgiving."

"Yeah," I answered. "It's raining and cold, and it's Florida! We'll be eating Thanksgiving dinner in a truck stop."

"Hey, the food is the best in the truck stops, and your gravy will be better than we could ever make. You've said so all along, and besides, what a great story to tell your grandchildren! Gotta run—I hear Daddy's car in the driveway!"

And that was the end of the conversation. Was she just trying to make me feel good?

We drove the rest of the morning and had lunch about two-thirty.

"We'll get a sandwich now and stop about seven tonight and get a turkey dinner then. How is that with you?" he contentedly asked.

Josh came from a family of boys. They had a flower shop, so holidays were mingled with working and delivering flowers, and dinner was squeezed in along the way. A family of girls makes a bigger fuss over holidays.

We entered the diner and ordered, and I asked the waitress for a piece of pumpkin pie.

"No, wait," Josh said. "Have it tonight with our dinner."

"I want it now."

"Nah, wait," he said affably. "We'll have pumpkin pie with our Thanksgiving dinner later."

"I want it now," I said like a stubborn kid.

He smiled at the waitress, baffled.

I wanted that pie now just because everyone at home was together. I looked at him, I looked at the waitress, and I walked out of the restaurant, leaving my sandwich and soda untouched. I went over to the truck and started to cry.

He came out and said, "Let's go." He didn't understand, didn't understand my tears. Well, neither did I. I didn't know what to say. We rode in silence. I felt the tears rolling down my face, and I couldn't explain it to him.

"I'm sorry if I did anything wrong," he said sincerely.

Him? I was the one who did something wrong! I reached for him across the seat, but I wanted to be even closer, so I climbed behind him and put my arms around his neck.

"It's not you, Josh. It's just that I'm not home for the holiday. Yet I want to be with you."

We drove until dark and pulled up at a truck stop. It was packed; I was surprised by how many people were not home for the holiday. We ordered our turkey dinner, and Josh reached for the phone on the table and said, "Why don't you call home."

Trying to be nonchalant, I said, "No, I'm with you." But he insisted, and I hesitated no longer.

I called Kathy's house, and the whole family passed the phone around, wishing us Happy Thanksgiving. Kathy's mother-in-law said, "I bet Josh is just thrilled to have you with him—he's usually alone on a holiday." I hadn't looked at it that way. I'd thought he was so self-reliant.

We got back in the truck, and he expertly maneuvered it out of a tight spot. I looked over at him and really noticed him—not just the muscled chest, the physical man I was attracted to, but *him*. I realized he understood me and brought me serenity like no one else. His hand reached over and rubbed the nape of my neck. I could have purred as the knotted muscles of the day relaxed, and I finally knew this was where I wanted to be.

Constance Conace

V
PATHFINDERS

*"Hell would be if God were to show me things
I could have accomplished
if only I had believed in myself."*

—Author unknown

PRAY TO GOD AND READ THE PAPER

I have always had a special view of love. Even as a ten-year-old, I remember, I believed in a kind of love that was eternal and powerful and unlike any of the relationships I had observed around me. Throughout my life, every fountain coin and birthday wish remained the same: "I pray that one day I will find true love and that it will last forever." There were times when I had almost given up, but even as I approached thirty, the wish remained fundamentally the same. I had been burned enough to be discouraged, but was hopeful enough to know in my heart that if I was patient and faithful, God would find me a husband to fulfill all my adolescent dreams. My mother always told me to stop trying so hard: love would come when I was not expecting it. Mom was right.

Before I was ready to be married, I knew I needed to clean up the stray ends of my life. The first step involved moving out of an apartment that was subject to seasonal flooding. The desire to move and be free of the worry of high tide was in my head, but I had not actually put thoughts into action. In fact, I ran around so much with work and friends and insignificant errands that I couldn't seem to find the time to buy a paper to look for a new place to live. Until one day I ran out of my apartment in the usual rush, only to trip over the morning paper. Not that odd, except for the fact that I don't subscribe to any morning paper. That day I picked it up and decided that if God was delivering a paper, maybe I was supposed to read it. I found three ads for promising apartments and one for sharing a house. I got two bizarre answering machine messages and hung up. I called the other two. One person, Paul, called back, and I arranged to meet him and possibly share his house. I don't know what I expected, but he was sweet and funny and didn't mind that I had a cat. He offered me a glass of orange juice, and we sat and got acquainted. I spoke longingly of my alma mater and found out that he had graduated from the same school. I suddenly flashed back to freshman orientation, when the speaker told us that 85 percent of Bucknell alumni married Bucknell graduates. I'd never forgotten that statistic. I looked at the house, I looked at the man, and I arranged to move in the next month. There was something in my heart that knew, and I was afraid to mention it to anyone for fear of breaking the spell. I moved in and made myself at home. We soon developed a breakfast routine and shared morning conversation. Sometimes we would watch television and talk until late at night. He teased me about my penchant for eating Ben & Jerry's ice cream for breakfast. I laughed at his ability to imitate Jimmy Stewart and Scooby-Doo. Eventually, I broke up with my current boyfriend, and he ended his relationship of the moment. I've been in his house for a year now, and we're engaged. Now we read the morning paper together.

Susan LaMaire

"Dream passionate dreams. Design their reality."
—CANDIS FANCHER

FLIGHT OF DESTINY

"Whatever do you think you're doing?" my mind screamed at me. "Who the hell do you think you are?"

I was in the middle of a flying lesson—one that was going so badly I burst into tears. The harder I tried to learn to fly the tiny single-engine airplane, the worse I got. I couldn't seem to do anything right!

It didn't help that my instructor was young and gorgeous and I had a crush on him. Not only did I want to succeed for me; I wanted to look brilliant, for him. But it was going so poorly that even he lost it and began yelling at me! After his first couple of words, I couldn't hear him anymore. All I could think of was: You're a fool to try to fly airplanes. After all, you're just a girl. You'll never get it!

As I drove home, all my doubts and self-loathing flooded to the surface. All the stupid things I'd done and said throughout my life now came to mind, and there seemed an overwhelming lot of them. My mind told me I was stupid, dumb, and ugly. What's more, I couldn't believe my arrogance at even *trying* to learn to fly! As if I had a hope of *ever* getting it! I cried bitter tears all the way home.

Amazingly enough, the next day at the appointed time, I got back into my car and drove to the airport. Convinced as I was of not being capable, I kept going. For you see, the passion in my soul was a runaway fire, and nothing—not even my negative self-talk—was going to stop me from becoming a flight instructor.

On my second lesson, when my instructor reviewed the basic maneuvers, I laughed in joy as I soared, wheeled, and wobbled all over the sky. Learning to talk on the radio was another challenge. In this world of male radio voices, I wanted to sound calm, cool, and professional. I worried about it so much that I stumbled all over myself trying to get the words out! But learning to land was the most important. When my instructor did it, it looked so easy. My turn came, and I floated and bumped. That night, I even dreamed, over and over, of awful landings. I was completely convinced that I was a lost cause, yet the following day, I planned to practice more landings. I flew in, and as we rolled down the runway, I realized that I had just made a landing so smooth that we hadn't even *felt* the touchdown. Success!

In hindsight, it all happened in baby steps. Almost before I knew it, I soloed. It was the most triumphant moment of my life. Not only did I do it all by myself, but I did it well. Even my mind chatter couldn't find fault. On every takeoff, I felt the freedom of my spirit disconnecting from the earth and becoming part of the universe.

That was twenty-one years ago—that mystical time when I began to learn to trust myself. In my earlier years, I used to fight the part of me that wasn't sweet, soft, and obedient. Now I appreciate every feisty quality about myself. And remember my self-talk about being stupid, dumb, and ugly? Well, I don't think so! My confidence is sky-high, and I've come to know the truth: I'm wonderful, special, talented, and perfect just the way I am. This discovery has given me compassion and respect, as I honor the beauty and perfection in other unique individuals everywhere. My inner peace and serenity pulsates so strongly that I know others sense it. Thank God I reached out for what I wanted.

As for my goal of becoming a flight instructor... I flew through that goal and beyond. I am now an international pilot for United Airlines. Weekly, I fly to Paris, London, and other magical places.

I am passionately living my dream!

ROBIN RYAN

FERN CAVE

Each year my sister and I take a weekend trip together to pursue our strong interest in birds and nature. This time she had talked me into going with her to the annual Bald Eagle Conference.

The weekend was an informative and entertaining mix of birding, lectures, and field trips. On the last day of the conference, we carpooled to a site called Fern Cave. The name made my skin crawl. All my life, I had suffered from claustrophobia so intense that at times I would not use elevators.

Our guide pulled up in the open desert and stopped his car. We all moved out into the frigid February air, then walked a short distance. I kept looking around my flat, barren surroundings, wondering where a cave might be. The high desert stretched for miles, covered with sagebrush and dusted by an icy, arid wind. The ranger stopped walking. As we approached him, I saw a yawning hole in the desert floor, covered by a wide steel grate.

The ranger bent down, picked a sprig of sage and poked it through his buttonhole, then removed a small leather medicine bag from his pocket and placed it around his neck. What was going on?

Our guide unlocked the grate and we descended into another world. As I crawled carefully down the ladder, the ranger's words echoed in my ears: "This was an ancient Modoc Indian holy place, used until 1873, when the Modoc people were sent to an Oklahoma reservation. Only recently did several Modoc medicine people return to Fern Cave."

We entered one end of a lava tube, where the roof had fallen in long ago. Below the opening was indeed a fern grotto, greenly lush and starkly out of place. The air had become heavy, humid, and warm. The ferns were beautiful and healthy, fed by the light from above, the nutrients from hapless rabbits, rodents, and snakes that had fallen in, and the water dripping from the cave roof. It was an amazing ecosystem: a full-size terrarium.

But even more amazing were the layer upon layer of pictographs that covered the walls near the opening in the cave. These were not secular drawings. This had been a cave for spirit quests and ceremonies of importance to the native people. The ranger told us that when the Modoc medicine people entered Fern Cave in the early nineties, they fell to their knees in awe and respect. The spirit images descended from the quarter-mile section of the lava tube beyond the chamber and moved gently into two circles. The grandmother spirits formed the inner circle. The outer circle was formed by warrior spirits.

We were given time to wander the cave on our own. Feeling like a voyeur, I self-consciously flashed my light on the mysterious pictographs around me. Shutting the light off, I moved into a large chamber where the roof of the cave grew to at least thirty feet in height. A peaceful, loving feeling enveloped me. It was dark and dense, like heavy, warm bedcovers on a cold winter's night. I stood in silent wonder at how I could feel so welcome in a place like this—a cave! Yet I felt surrounded by love, and the feeling of spiritual presence was unmistakable. I wanted nothing more than to sit and drink in this thick, pungent, loving air.

Gradually, people began making their way back up the ladder, as I stood silently in the bowels of the cave, in tears. My heart ached with longing. I didn't want to leave, wanted to spend the rest of my life here. Finally, it became apparent that I was the last one left, and our group leader motioned to me. I struggled to pull myself back up the ladder. As I reached the surface, I required assistance to avoid falling backward.

I stood on the edge of the cave opening and attempted to adjust to the desert world. The bitter February wind whipped by as the sagebrush rustled all around. Solemnly and silently, we walked back to our vehicles.

I have never completely returned from Fern Cave. On several occasions since then, visitors to my home have told me they sensed others in the room with us. As the familiar feeling of overwhelming love surrounds me, I know the grandmother spirits are present.

Sharon Kinder

LETTER TO TIM

I knew Tim by sight. Or rather by sound. Everybody in Central School did. Not that he was loud—although even when he was eleven, his voice had that ringing, penetrating quality. He was an outrageous joker-punster even then. As far as I knew, he wasn't aware of me.

One afternoon, though, we ended up in a classroom together with my friend Sue. Tim chatted with us, all the while lifting used staples off the chalk tray and plunking them into an old Band-Aid box. I watched him do this for a few seconds, then blurted, "Why are you doing that?"

He shrugged. "Same reason you were keeping that notebook of animal names last year."

I stared at him, forgetting the Band-Aid box. The previous year, I'd started jotting down my various pets' names—a more ambitious undertaking than it sounds, since my brother Gary and I were always dragging cats home from my grandparents' farm. Probably fifty or sixty of them had passed through our lives by that time. I'd been afraid of forgetting even the littlest kittens, who'd been with us maybe a few weeks before distemper picked them off. Then other kids had begun giving me pets' names, and I'd written those down too. Why, I don't know, except that even then I was caught up in the poetry of names and naming, just as now the names of herbs and quilt patterns create a vivid magic for me. But that afternoon in the darkened classroom, waiting for the bus, I was just floored that a strange boy had noticed my oddball scribbling.

In high school, we met up again and became good friends while he chased after one of the girls I hung out with and a couple of the others chased after him. We talked on the phone some and in our sophomore English classroom a lot. We acted in a couple of one-act plays together. And once he gave me a poem he'd clipped out of the newspaper—a simple, moving piece that I kept among my papers for years. I don't remember all the words, but it was about having "wise eyes."

We drifted apart, then happened across each other after our freshman year of college and started dating. Eventually, we married and had Marissa, a child with all her dad's quick restlessness and imaginativeness. We were never a picture-perfect couple. I used to joke that we'd be arguing with each other about dentures and walkers when Marissa finally shipped us off to a convalescent home. But we'd both get teary-eyed and sniffly over the dumbest scenes in movies and laugh when we caught each other doing it. And there were those moments when soul met soul and we saw with each other's eyes. "We're more alike than you realize," he once said to me; and he was right. We were friends, fellow questers, and part of each other's childhood, with more memories than we could ever shake free of. Staples in a Band-Aid box. And he believed in my dream of being a writer, even on days when I couldn't quite make myself believe in it.

"If I've done nothing else in my life," he'd say, "I've tried to be supportive of your writing.... I believe you have what it takes to be a great writer."

That early Tuesday in July was one of those "the wall looked at me wrong" kind of days. Nothing seemed to be going right. Then I had a call from an editor, who bubbled over with enthusiasm about a piece I'd put a lot of myself into. I was glowing when I put down the phone. "Wait until Tim hears about this!" I exulted.

He never did. His van skidded on a slick all too familiar road on his way home and flipped over, hitting a pole and killing him instantly.

A few days later, we buried him in the wooded little cemetery behind the house that overlooked the mountain he'd loved. In what seemed a parody of our wedding, nine years earlier, the brother who'd walked me down the aisle guided me to my husband's graveside. The sun touched the cherry coffin, bringing out the red glints in the wood, and I thought: What a beautiful coffin! And the thought, odd as it was, stayed with me throughout the service. When it was over, I stooped down and kissed the lid—I'd been unable to look at what was left of him.

I could not let him go into the ground without some sign and held out my hand for the spade. The funeral director shook his head gently and made a motion with his hand: You don't have to do this. But I did. And afterward, I bent down and kissed the lid one last time, dirt and all.

"Let me watch you go with the sun in my eyes," Diana Ross sings in "Touch Me in the Morning." I remember listening to that line with a good friend back in high school; we'd turned to look at each other, moved out of our adolescent egocentrism by the pain and the poetry of the words. Well, I had watched my love and friend go with the sun in my eyes, all right. But the love wasn't dead: It was as close as my heart and stronger than death.

For weeks afterward, I could not write. Nor could I let all the tears out. Finally, one night a poem appeared, brought into being out of my pain. And it told me that somewhere in the battered, darkened house of my being was a person who could still flame into feeling. I kept a journal. It helped, though the words still came haltingly, as though I were recovering from a stroke. But they came back to me, and that was all I cared.

"You must do that thing you think you cannot do," insisted Eleanor Roosevelt, who overcame great shyness and personal pain to do great things for other people. The one thing that I knew I had to do for my soul to heal—the one thing I couldn't quite bring myself to do—was to write about Tim's death. Then my counselor said to me, "Maybe you could write a good-bye letter to Tim."

So this is my goodbye letter to the smart-mouthed kid with a Band-Aid box, the boy who surprised me with the poem about wise eyes, the blunt, sensitive, playful man who gave me Marissa, laughter, and his belief in me. And as I've sat here writing, the tears have finally found me and freed the words and feelings trapped under the rubble. I have a voice again. It's a different voice. I don't know if it—or my eyes, for that matter

—are any wiser. But it is capable of greater depth, openness, and, I hope, compassion. Out of great pain, a new voice has been born.

T. J. BANKS

AND BABY MAKES THREE

I step from the shower, wrap the towel around me, and stare down at my big Himalayan cat, Sheba. Her wise sapphire eyes contemplate the tears streaming down my cheeks, onto her luxuriant white fur. I sense her telling me, "Mom, I know what you really want is a kid with two feet, but what you got was a kitty with four paws. If you do a good job with me, the word is you'll get your kid."

I prayed that night and every night that my cat was right. Coming as I had from a violent, dysfunctional family lacking real love, it was just not enough that I'd become a successful entrepreneur and traveled the world. After passing the fortieth year of my unmarried existence, I craved what was missing in my life: someone I could love and someone to love me back.

A tenacious inner voice prodding me along, I began the adoption process. Seven years dragged by. Finally, I got the heart-stopping phone call that told me that I qualified for a baby girl soon to be born in Las Vegas, Nevada. I would turn forty-eight one week after her birth. *You have to be nuts, Donna,* a part of me was thinking. *It takes herculean energy to raise a child, and you're too damned old to go through sleepless nights and the financial burden of a college education. And if something happens to you, what then?*

Even friends familiar with my struggle to adopt warned me of the downside and seemed reluctant to offer encouragement. And yet I refused to be discouraged. I passionately wanted a child. Then Sheba snuggled up beside me, and her big blues seemed to say, "Go for it. I love ya, and so will What's-her-name."

When I brought Mariah Chelsea Hartley home, my world turned upside down, but I was ecstatic. It had really happened. My baby girl was home in my arms. Yes, there were sleepless nights, gallons of formula, dozens of dirty diapers, and the haunting insecurity of motherhood. Mariah's smiles blossomed forth, and the unconditional love shining in her eyes became my happiness.

The months flew by, and I struggled against my tight work schedule to spend every moment I could observing Mariah's baby miracles: a hand brushing my cheek, gurgles of delight, chubby miniature arms wrapping around my neck, and the utter joy of hearing "Mama" from rosebud lips crinkled up in a smile. As a new mother, I've learned that each day unleashes new experiences and a reason to show patience and tolerance for the tiny being you love.

And what does my furry cat princess feel about this invasion of her territory by cries in the night and curious poking fingers? I can tell you, we really are a family. At least that's the way I understood it after I returned from the grocery store, pulled into the garage, and saw Mariah asleep in the back seat. Since she was in eye view of my kitchen, I left the car door open and didn't disturb her. Sheba gave me her "Where's the kid?" meow and proceeded to search the house. A while later, I found Sheba curled up next to my sleeping daughter. I knew I had made the right choice. Even Sheba knew. There was no doubt as to what my feline friend was saying this time: "Hey, Mom, and baby makes three."

DONNA HARTLEY

*"Taking care of yourself does not require a lot of time—
just meticulous timing."*
—Author unknown

IT'S ABOUT TIME

As children, we're instinctively aware of the simple, natural rhythms of the earth. Growing up without electricity or TV, I would often watch the drama of a thunderstorm rolling across the South Dakota prairie instead. Excitedly I'd wait for the ominous-looking clouds and the electrifying bolts of light in the night sky. My father would say, "After you see the lightning, listen for the thunder and count—you'll know how far away the storm is."

Country life was full of cycles and rhythms. Knowing the right time for plowing, planting, and harvesting was critical to a dry-land farmer. Understanding the breeding of cows at a particular time ensured calves' coming into a world of spring grass and not winter snow. It all made sense and seemed like part of a master plan.

When the time came for me to leave the farm and attend the big-city university, I found that people woke up to alarms instead of the breaking morning light. Appointments and schedules were not in harmony with one's body clock but made to suit someone else's convenience and efficiency. The weather, the seasons, and the true time of day were virtually ignored. I felt disoriented and out of sync.

Struggling for balance, I took some classes in chronobiology (the study of time and the body), which was a relatively new science in the sixties. I learned about a symphony of rhythms in nature, including those in my own body. It was amazing to find that there was a "best time" to do almost everything: there's an ebb and flow, a waxing and waning of our alertness, our strength, and our energy. A familiarity I had felt with the "master plan" of my childhood returned. I managed my schedule to optimize my performance at school.

On one spring break, I was enthusiastically telling my father about the research being done at chronobiological labs on the timing of cancer treatments. My father listened patiently and replied, "Cancer cells are like weeds. Every farmer knows that weed killer sprayed on crops at one time of day will kill the weeds and the plants will be resistant. At another time of day, they'll both die."

After college, the corporate life promised me money, travel, and a career; my interest in things like chronobiology faded. I took a job in computer sales and became progressively detached from my emotions and feelings as I focused on quotas and achievements. My boss would say, "Whatever it takes," and I would do whatever it took, at any personal cost. I came to find later that the cost was greater than I'd imagined.

After several years of success, I had a growing bank account and a failed marriage, and my father had passed away. I had no one to perform for or impress. I could feel nothing: pain, anger, love, or happiness. I was out of balance, out of sync, off kilter, and alone.

And then I was diagnosed with breast cancer. Dealing with this crisis knocked me off the corporate gerbil wheel and put me in touch with deeper feelings once again. I longed for the synchronicity and balance I'd enjoyed as a child.

It had been twenty-five years since I paid attention to the research on cancer treatments at school. Now I was desperate to know what the researchers had learned while I was absent from "life." My first call for information was not to the cancer hot line but to my former university professor. He told me that top researchers had found that the time of the month a biopsy is performed, and the time of day the treatment is given, are significant to long-term survival. Specifically, he said:

- Breast cancer surgery may be 30–40 percent more effective if performed midway in the menstrual cycle.
- Treatments given at the right time of day are more potent and may cause fewer side effects.

My diagnosis was a wake-up call. It tuned me in and reminded me that when we get intimate with our bodies' internal timing, we can sense what's coming—like the thunder before the storm.

Now I exercise at the best time for my body, eat at the right time, even make love and schedule business meetings at the optimal time. My doctor says my prognosis for long-term survival is great.

Country wisdom tells us that there's a right and a wrong time for most everything we do.

I have a friend who's been happily married for thirty-five years. She gets up at five A.M. He goes to bed at four A.M. She laughingly says, "Our love is always hot, and the bed is never cold." Another friend writes songs or vacuums nude at two A.M. Early-morning people hit the ground running, breathe in the fresh air of dawn, and wonder what's wrong with the rest of us. I found that my best time of day was often wasted in traffic on the way home from work.

"Making hay while the sun shines" makes sense whether you're on the farm or in the city. We must find the opportunity to live in balance by matching our efforts with the flow of our natural rhythms. It's about time for you too!

NANCY KIERNAN

VI
FREE AT LAST

"The soul should always stand ajar, ready to welcome the ecstatic experience."

—Emily Dickinson

*"A workable measure of your progress
is how fast you can get free when you are stuck
and how many ways you know to get free."*
—Kathlyn Hendricks

A Walk on the Wild Side

At last, a few days all to myself, away from the stress of the city.

"Watch out for hanta virus," had warned my husband, the noncamper.

"Remember the forest belongs to the wild things that live there," had chided my son, who respects wild things.

"Be r-e-a-l-l-y careful of the Big Bad Wolf," had chirped my five-year-old granddaughter.

"Zip-a-dee-doo-dah, zip-a-dee-ay!" In a closed car, going fifty-eight miles an hour up Route 5 away from Los Angeles, my fifty-eight-year-old voice sounded pretty good.

Through the Grapevine and on to Bakersfield. No rush. No worries.

At Giant Forest Lodge, a friendly woman handed me directions to my cabin. A sign behind her caught my eye: DO NOT FEED THE BEARS. "Who would want to feed a bear?" I said.

At seven A.M., I awoke to the gentle sounds of birds. No lunches to pack, no meetings to plan.

I pulled on my sweatsuit, brushed my teeth, put on sunscreen and mosquito repellent. With a water bottle in my backpack, I was ready to experience the tranquillity of the forest.

MORROW ROCK, a sign read. I stood tall, looked up the trail, and accepted the invitation.

I reached down to pick up two walking sticks. Waving them over my head like a warrioress, I called out to the ghost of my childhood. "I am Jane, you are Tarzan." My brothers and I spent most of our spare time in the woods near our house, imitating childhood heroes.

"We are marching to Pretoria, Pretoria, Pretoria!"

The sky is a great audience. Swinging my sticks back and forth made me feel powerful.

As I walked on, the branches of a sequoia ahead of me began shaking. Its cones fell like hail on the forest floor. The barrage didn't make sense. It wasn't windy. I couldn't see anything. Yet it shook violently. I put my walking sticks over my head and ran through.

The cones continued to fall behind me as I sat down on a fallen log. I had been walking more than two hours and felt hot and tired. It was about nine-thirty. I opened my backpack and took out my water.

I noticed a bluebird, a meandering butterfly, and some half-eaten red berries on a thorny bush nearby. I heard what seemed like the intrusive sound of a passing car in the distance and what I assumed were park rangers building something. About five minutes went by; I was thinking of taking a nap.

Suddenly a loud thump ripped away my serenity and catapulted me into life-threatening danger. A black bear dropped out of the tree I'd just passed and began walking toward me on all fours. I felt so dumb. No wonder the tree was shaking and the berries were half eaten!

My insides started screaming. But my mouth wouldn't move. My body wanted to run, yet I couldn't outrun a bear.

I thought I was having a heart attack. A bad childhood case of rheumatic fever had left me with an irregular heartbeat. "Nothing to worry about," my doctor said. "Just leaky valves." Wrong! I definitely had something to worry about.

Terrified, I turned my back on the bear and staggered in the direction of where I thought I had heard the passing car.

My thoughts raced back and forth, up and down, like a television picture on the fritz. I knew everyone would be mad at me if I got eaten by a bear.

I walked with fierce determination. Waved my sticks over my head. And sang.

"Whenever I feel afraid, I hold my head erect, and whistle a happy tune . . ."

Off the path, weaving in and out of obstacles, I sloshed into marshland. Frantically I looked over my shoulder, hoping the bear was gone. No luck! He was twenty feet away, slowly closing in. Shock waves rolled through my body. My knees felt weak.

A fallen tree appeared out of nowhere, to create a forty-foot bridge over the marsh. Could I balance on it? I'd been a dancer . . . thirty years ago. Could I cross and get beyond the marsh to where I was hoping against hope there was a road and people . . . and escape? I stepped up and prayed Mr. Bear would be too big for this small balance beam.

Knees shaking, I teetered across the tree . . . slipped and fell . . . scrambled back up and shakily went on. The bear's footfalls competed with my pounding heart. He was on the tree. Perfectly balanced. Fifteen feet away. Barnum & Bailey would have hired him in a flash.

African drums began to beat wildly inside my heart. I wondered why a search-and-rescue party didn't carry me out of this morning nightmare. Where was Tarzan of the jungle when I needed him?

Suddenly I heard a deep, booming voice inside my head. *"Do you want to live?"* It was jarring. I wondered if, indeed, I really had a choice. I reached the end of the log and jumped off.

"Do you want to live?" continued to reverberate inside me. The voice helped me put the brakes on fear and terror and take an angel's flight into determination.

"Yes, yes, yes!" I answered. I turned around and angrily stared the bear straight in the eye. I pounded my walking sticks over my head and shouted: "I will not miss my daughter's acting debut. I will not miss my son's cooking at his new restaurant. I will not miss my husband's new musical show. I will not miss my granddaughter's next birthday. Now, *go away."*

I turned, tore through undergrowth, bushes scratching, snagging my clothes. I went on as if the bear were still behind me, climbed a twenty-foot embankment, and, too numb to move, watched a car drive by. I looked back. I couldn't see the bear, but I could feel him in the brush, his eyes still following me.

Frantically, I flagged down another car and scrambled into the metal womb, grateful to be alive. Feeling a growing surge of new strength and joy—born out of having had a close call and been given a precious gift—I started humming under my breath: "Zip-a-dee-doo-dah, zip-a-dee-ay."

JUDITH MORTON FRASER

*"You and I can live in a world of enchantment,
but only when we feed
and care for our soul."*
—Deborah Olive

THE WARM FUZZY HOSTILE GROUP

"Two hundred people will be attending, and you need to know that they all hate each other, hate their work, and don't want to hear what you have to say. And by the way, we are a nonprofit organization, and we don't have a lot of money to pay you."

I stood in shock as I heard myself say, "I would be honored to speak at your regional conference."

I hung up the phone and proceeded to have a complete temper tantrum.

"I didn't volunteer for this," I yelled to God, as I stomped around my kitchen.

"Oh, yes you did, Jody," I clearly heard. "When you left your corporate job, you said you would teach the world Soul Purpose Principles if I would support you. Well, I am supporting you, and I need you to teach *my* truths to these folks."

"OK, God," I mumbled. "Who am I to argue with you? I will do it, but I don't like it."

"You don't have to like it; you just have to be willing to serve," I was gently reminded.

The invitation to speak came in January for an April event. For three months I jokingly referred to this opportunity as the "hostile group." For three months I stewed over the fear of speaking to an angry, unwilling group. For three months I visualized dodging the raw eggs and rotten tomatoes I was sure they were going to throw at me. For three months I kept trying to rewrite my keynote speech, to sound more corporate than spiritual. Finally, the day had arrived.

"Even though we have not met, and even though some of you may not want to be here," I started out tentatively, "and even though some of you may not want to hear what I am about to say, I know four things about you that you will agree with."

Smiling faces beamed back at me. Hmm. Silently I laughed at myself, thinking this was not the response I had prepared myself for.

"Every one of you here wants four things," I continued. "And if you had these four things, you would tell me you were living a soulful and purposeful life. *One:* one hundred percent harmonious relationships. *Two:* a vibrant, healthy body. *Three:* an expanding sense of prosperity. *Four:* to be living your soul purpose and making a difference."

Enthusiastically, they nodded. "In order to create these experiences, you need to know a few things about your Soul," I suggested, my confidence having returned.

- *The Soul demands to be free.* Freedom, by definition, means: Not being dependent on others. Being self-reliant. Not being determined by anything beyond the Soul's own nature or being.

    Americans are not feeling free. According to the Center for Disease Control, 750,000 Americans will die of heart disease in 1997. What is even more interesting is that more heart attacks happen between the hours of seven and nine A.M. Monday morning.
- *The Soul yearns for the silent pause.* We each have 1,440 minutes in a twenty-four-hour period. After years of helping people discover their Soul's purpose, the most common statement I hear is: "I don't know." In order to discover why we exist and what to do with our creative

energies, we *must* sit quietly and listen. Just two minutes a day, or more. Great wisdom emerges out of a silent moment.

- *The Soul delights in the tribal pulse.* We all need and want to belong. Living a soulful life requires us to take ruthless inventory of the people we hang around with. Are they positive, supportive, and nurturing? Are they willing to tell us the truth, even when we don't want to hear it? Are they willing to let us tell them the truth, even when they don't want to hear it? Are the people in our lives spiritually focused, and if not, why would we choose to hang out in a negative, degrading tribe?
- *The destiny of every Soul is to present its finest creative expression to humanity.* Our Soul, that quiet, shy, powerful, unique part of us, holds our physical temple, our body, so that we may express our own set of talents and skills. It is our very destiny to say *yes* to our greatness and boldly step out into the world, sharing and serving humanity in our own unique way. We simply will not be happy until we do.

As I concluded my presentation, I received roaring applause, many accolades, and thanks. Riding the elevator up to the lobby allowed me a precious moment of quiet.

"OK, God, you win. I surrender my will to you. Show me where and with whom you want me to serve next. I will speak, teach, and write about *your* Soul-purpose principles. And thank you for the opportunity to speak with the fabulous warm fuzzy 'hostile group.' "

Things are not always what they seem. I now know that what we resist in life is often our biggest opportunity to learn and grow!

JODY STEVENSON

CREATE YOUR OWN
HEAVEN TODAY

When I learned that my favorite aunt had died, I was horror-struck. Her death came as a shock because my mother had just written to say she was doing much better. To make matters worse, my family didn't tell me about her death for a week, because I was away and they "didn't want to worry me." That compounded the grief. When I finally found out, I shed powerful tears for days, as if to send my aunt Bea higher and higher into heaven.

One night during that period of grief, I had a dream. The feeling was so strong and the picture so vivid that I can still see and feel it today. In the dream, I was standing in heaven, in front of a beautiful English cottage. Set back in a gorgeous garden, with a stone path leading to the front door, the cottage itself was covered with roses. A white picket fence surrounded it.

There I was, standing in front of the fence. The setting was very tranquil. I had a deep sense of inner peace such as I had never experienced before. It was all-embracing. I didn't want it to go away.

Out of nowhere, a figure stood in front of me.

He radiated the same incredible peace. I asked him, "What's this all about?"

The answer I got back really surprised me. "Welcome," He said. "You can stay here too if you would like, but you have to follow one rule."

"What's that?" I asked.

"You can use only positive words and positive thoughts about everyone and everything," he said. "If you don't, you'll drop right out of here."

He didn't say where I would go, but I had a feeling I knew.

I wondered if I could discipline my mind to stay that positive.

One thing I knew for sure was that I wanted that tranquillity more than anything. I wanted to stay.

I was about to say yes when I woke up.

The impact of that experience was so strong that I remember it as if it were yesterday. I tell audiences I speak to: "Think what life could be like if we used only positive words and positive thoughts."

Here's the real question: Do we have the power to create heaven on earth? I *know* we do. We can do it together—thought by thought.

CHRISTINE HARVEY

YOU ARE MY BROTHER

Can *love dispel* evil? *Can peace overcome* war? I had always argued so, taking the moral high road. "Love and forgiveness is all well and good," some friends would argue, "but what place do they have if *you're* the one under attack?" Still I persisted in believing love has a place and a power of which we may not always be aware.

Not long ago, while attending a medical conference in Philadelphia, I returned to my hotel room to freshen up before a late-night committee meeting. Locking the door behind me, I entered the bathroom. I quickly combed my hair and bent over the sink to wash my face. As I closed my eyes and splashed cold water over my skin, I instinctively knew I was not alone. Jerking my body up, I watched in the mirror's reflection as a hand reached out and ripped back the shower curtain behind me. Reeling, I barely had time to react before a man dressed in army fatigues leapt from the shower and pinned me against the sink. I screamed as he clasped my arms with one hand and started to shut the bathroom door with the other.

He grabbed me, and we were suddenly face-to-face. As I looked at him full on, I realized I would never win a war of strength against him. In that moment, my mind and my body seemed to go in different directions. With my heart beating wildly, I continued to scream. Yet another part of me felt a strange peacefulness and began speaking to him in my mind. Locking eyes with him, I started repeating over and over in my head the phrase: "This must be a mistake. You are my brother. There can be nothing but love between us. You cannot hurt me. This is a mistake. You are my brother. There can be nothing but love between us. This is a mistake...."

"This is a mistake," he said suddenly, and he released me

and slowly backed away. Shaking his head, as if dazed, he repeated, "This is a mistake," and he turned and fled out the door.

KATHI J. KEMPER

THE JOURNEY HOME

Our destination is Troyes, a city in the Champagne region, about ninety minutes from Paris. I stare out the window of the train, hands clenched tightly over the package on my lap. My husband, Tom, and I are bringing my mother's ashes home.

Last June, eleven months ago, I drove Mom to the doctor for her monthly exam. As always, she was pronounced in excellent health. Took her diabetes medications, her blood pressure pills. Didn't smoke or drink. Followed a careful diet. At age seventy-seven, she seemed likely to live for another ten or twenty years. So why, after lunch, did our conversation turn to death?

I was standing at the kitchen sink, washing dishes. Heaven only knows how the subject came up, but I mentioned that when I died, I wanted to be cremated. Mom, drying dishes, cocked her head, considering this.

"Maybe I do too," she said suddenly.

"Really? How come?" I was interested. It occurred to me that we had never discussed this part of living before. Mom's answer was typically French: realistic, sensible.

"Well, at first it sounds yucky"—*yuqui*—"but so is being buried, when you think about it. Being cremated is sanitary. And it's cheap! I saw on *20/20* that funeral directors rip you off"—*reep you uff*—"and I don't want you wasting money on me after I croak." We laughed. At that moment, the prospect of her croaking seemed very far away.

"And where do you want your ashes to go?" I asked her, already knowing the answer.

"France!" she exclaimed. "In my own backyard." Mom arrived in the U.S. as a war bride fifty years ago, admired her adopted homeland, was a proud naturalized citizen—but Gallic blood flowed in her veins, and she remained French to her toes.

Then she looked doubtful. "Can you bring ashes to France? Is it legal?"

"Oh, sure," I promised casually, not really knowing, but who cared? If it was what Mom wanted, it was what I would do—someday, a long time from now.

But how could we know that a month later a tumor would show up in her liver? And that soon she'd be too weak to care for herself, chemotherapy shrinking her already tiny frame to eighty pounds?

Six months later, she was gone.

I'm a therapist by profession. I thought I understood bereavement. But now I learned firsthand about the mother-daughter connection. No matter how much other love you have in your life, when your mother dies, your world is cut out from under you. For weeks I lived in a daze: lost, rootless, terrifyingly alone. This despite a loving husband, despite my loving friends. I found I contained an inexhaustible supply of tears. I wondered if I would ever feel all right again.

On the train, I am edgy, short-tempered. I hold the box containing her ashes, wrapped in a silk scarf she brought from France fifty years ago. Next to me is a city map of Troyes, my camera and extra film, and Kleenex. Lots of Kleenex.

I keep remembering my last trip here, to visit Mom's sisters, and how wonderful it was. I feel the tears welling up behind my eyes, as I imagine myself scattering the ashes. I keep my eyes fixed on the passing scenery, determined not to think about it. No need to feel this awful more than once.

Rue Lachat is a thin, dusty alley, ending in a cul-de-sac. We walk to the very end. There is the stone cottage owned by Mom's family for over one hundred years. There is the green-painted gatepost, paint flaking now. The gate is wired shut.

My aunts sold the house to the city over twenty years ago. It has sat vacant ever since. The last time we were here, we didn't dare do more than study the property from the outside.

Tom undoes the wire easily, and we step through a gate. To our left, a stone fence, at least six meters high, surrounds the property. A long path trails along the fence. We follow it to the end. A wooden gate, leading to the garden, is at the end of the path. Lifting the crossbar, we push the gate open and step inside to Mom's backyard.

It's an oasis, dazzling in the sun. Everything is pale green, the new springtime leaves tender and glossy—overgrown now, a jumble of ivy, of weeds, of buttercups, of fruit trees gone wild.

I have heard about this yard my entire life. I walk slowly through the greenery, touching plants, caressing the tiny apples forming on the trees. Silent, except for birdcalls, the drowsy hum of a bee.

My head is humming, filled with my mother. In my mind's eye, I see her little hands gesturing, watch her eyes gleam, see her wide, guileless smile. Her voice, her dainty accent, is so clear in my ears.

"Your grandfather loved birds. He used to sit on his chair in the yard, with his wooden leg propped on a stool—and sparrows would come and perch on it! . . .

"Your grandmother could grow anything. All the vegetables we ate she grew. During the war, all we had was rutabagas. The Nazis confiscated everything else. Lucky for us they didn't like rutabagas!"

So now here I am. Here on the site of a lifetime's worth of stories. My ancestral home. I'm the fourth generation, the last of my mother's line.

Finally, I kneel down, unzip my tote bag, lift out my precious burden.

"Welcome home, Mom," Tom says quietly.

"I promised I'd bring you back," I whisper, weeping. Just a little.

I poke a hole in the bag of ashes, shake a little dust onto the ground. It scatters lightly, lands on the pale-green leaves. I watch, fascinated. So quickly, it becomes part of the landscape, part of the yard. And then my leaden mood evaporates. I've been dreading this moment for months, and now it's here, and it's not awful. In fact, it's wonderful. She's here, she's home. I can feel Mom over my shoulder, encouraging me. *Let's geet theese show on ze road!*

Suddenly lighthearted, I rise to my feet, move out of the yard, hurry down the path to the main gate. Sprinkle some ash on the doorpost. Sprinkle a little in the mailbox. Sprinkle some over the path as I return to the garden. A forty-two-year-old Tinker Bell, scattering fairy dust.

"Ma, that's you all over," I say cheerfully.

Filled with joyous contentment, I feel her smiling behind me, feel my aunts, my grandparents, my great-grandmother, laughing at my performance. Death isn't forever, they're saying. We are. So are you.

In the middle of the garden, I hold the bag straight out in front of me, and I begin to spin, a slow circle. A sudden breeze touches the bag, catches the ashes, pulls them out, swirls them around me in a silver mist.

"Au revoir, Maman!" I shout.

"Bon voyage!"

"Je t'aime!" I scream. *I love you!*

The ashes dance in the breeze. The sun blazes overhead. I am laughing. Inside, I am lighter than air.

MARIE HEGEMAN

ME, MYSELF, AND I

If you've never truly discovered your own personal strength and worth as an independent woman, try traveling to an unfamiliar city alone.

I visited Minneapolis recently on business—I, a nearly native Texan, who's never experienced subzero temperatures. Several friends and family members had warned me how cold it is up there in the middle of January, how dangerous it is to be outside, and how my ears would fall off if I spent more than one minute in the cold. Sure, I listened—I'm always ready to take advice from those more knowledgeable than I am.

On the other hand, if I spent all my free time in the hotel, I'd never get to experience this beautiful city. So on my second day in the Twin Cities, I drove out to a suburb about twenty minutes from my hotel, to visit my former pastor's new church. Yep, I got lost, just as tourists do in a strange city when they get the wrong directions. But I discovered Hopkins, Minnesota—one of the quaintest cities I've ever seen. Hopkins is really a mixture of suburb and small town. Better yet, it snowed the entire hour I spent looking for the church. I've always wanted to live in a place where it snowed for Christmas, and even though Christmas was over, I pretended I was traveling to my family's home to spend the holiday in a snow-covered house with a snow-covered yard.

That afternoon, after finally finding the church and going to lunch with the pastor and his family, I checked out the Mall of America. Since I'm from Dallas, I'm used to seeing huge malls, but this was the Galleria times three and then some. It was possibly one of the most enjoyable adventures I've ever had. Being alone, I could walk as quickly or as slowly as I wanted. I could stop in any store I wanted and stay there for as long as I liked. I ended up spending three fun-filled hours in the mall, and then I decided to leave without having to ask if that was OK with my companion.

Don't get me wrong. I love spending time shopping and frolicking with friends and family. But this was a chance for me just to get away by myself and discover how much fun *I* am to be with.

You see, if I had been too afraid of the snow and the ice and the subzero temperatures, I'd never have discovered the warmth and beauty of this wonderful city, or how capable I am of getting around without anyone's help. Next time I go, though, I'll try to book the trip for June.

STEPHANIE LAURIDSEN

MODELING FOR LIFE

One late-summer day during my eleventh year, Mother and I spent a morning on a whirlwind shopping spree for back-to-school clothes. This was a rare event. Mom had a chronic illness and didn't often feel well enough to spend a day shopping. But on this particular day she seemed energized, as was I.

Mom treated me to lunch in the department store's restaurant. As we entered the dining area, I noticed elegant models sauntering from table to table, wearing the latest fall fashions. Since this was the prime buying season for school clothes, I wondered aloud why there were no preteen and teen models.

Impressed with my idea, Mother encouraged me to talk with someone. By the time dessert was served, she convinced me not only that my idea was great but that I should be one of those models!

I felt excited and scared. Her encouragement gave me confidence, and I actually began to believe in my idea and in myself. Mom's enthusiasm did not stop there; she persuaded me to talk to the store manager. Even though my stomach was churning, I was ready to apply for my first job!

Now, I should tell you I wasn't a willowy preteen version of Brooke Shields. No, I was short, a little chubby, bespectacled, and freckled—maybe cute but definitely not classic model material. Yet Mom's reassurance had convinced me I was beautiful and capable in that moment.

As the elevator doors closed, sending us up to the manager's office, I hesitated again. "Do you really think this is a good idea?" I asked.

In that moment, my mother spoke words that come back to me often—words that have changed the course of my life more than once. "What have you got to lose? You'll be no worse off if he says no. And maybe, just maybe, he'll say yes!"

So, refocused and inspired, I proceeded. When the elevator doors opened, I marched straight up to the secretary's desk and asked to see the store manager. The secretary hesitated, then let the manager know I wanted to see him. Before long, we were ushered into his office. As I sat across from him at his desk, I confidently explained that he had an opportunity to create more sales by showcasing back-to-school preteen and teen fashions this time of year. He listened politely and with interest. When I said I wanted to model, he gave me a job application, saying he would consider my suggestion.

While he never did call me, the next summer the department store ran a search for teens to model in the restaurant for a back-to-school fashion showing! In truth, I didn't really care that I was not selected. I had my reward. Mom gave me a gift that has endured a lifetime. Although she died a few years later, when I was fifteen, Mom's spirit is always with me when I face scary life situations.

Mom taught me it was safe to take risks, to believe in myself, and most important—to ask for what I want!

JOEANN FOSSLAND

VII

MOMENTS OF TRUTH

"Truth is the only safe ground to stand upon."

—Elizabeth Cady Stanton

WE ARE ALL CONNECTED
◦❦◦

While a junior at the University of Minnesota, I took a much-needed vacation to Mexico. I was tired. Tired in the way that only bartending full time at night while taking seventeen credits a quarter can make you. I went by myself, leaving my boyfriend and my books behind with the snowdrifts. I didn't want to meet anyone. I didn't want to party. I didn't even want to talk. I just wanted to stare. Sit on a beach and stare at the waves. Maybe poke around some ruins and stare at them too.

So when I kept bumping into the same gringo all over the Yucatán peninsula, I ignored it. I took the ferry to Isla Mujeres to stare at the phosphorescent fish, and he happened to be with the group waiting for the boat back to the mainland. I caught sight of him among the market tables at Mérida, where serapes and silver bangles were sold. I knew he wasn't following me, and I knew he must have noticed me, just as I couldn't help but notice him. Still, in need of rest and separation from people, I avoided eye contact with the ever-present gringo.

After climbing around the temples of Tulum, I climbed aboard a crowded bus for my return trip. I squeezed through the aisles toward the back and spied a perch on the edge of a seat that already had two people. The bus lurched onward, and I found myself sinking deep into thought. Even though I'd been surrounded for days by unfamiliar people, I realized we are all connected in some form. At that point, I looked up, to see seated next to me none other than the gringo!

We gave up trying to ignore each other. This was obviously kismet. The conversation came easily as we decided to become instant friends. We reached Cancún in a festive mood and headed for a lively little cantina with colored lights and palm trees.

After a satisfying dinner, a shared flan, and two cups of coffee, the gringo suddenly said, "Hey, what's your name?" We didn't even know each other's names! "Jean Wenzel," I said. A strange expression crossed his face. "What?" he asked, even though I was sure he'd heard me. "Jean Wenzel," I said again, enunciating very clearly.

He just looked at me. I looked at him. Finally, to break the odd spell that seemed to have come over him, I prompted, "What's yours?" He didn't reply, but he reached into his bag and pulled out his wallet and flipped it open to his driver's license. Yes, we really are all connected—his name was Gene Wenzel.

JEAN WENZEL

THE "WRITE" MATCH

This had not been an ordinary day for me. I looked at the lighted clock as it tick-tocked its way to an ungodly three A.M. My husband, Harold, was oblivious to my tossing and turning. He couldn't possibly imagine my anxiety.

Normally, I have no concerns on the cruises I take. My handwriting expertise becomes entertainment, and the lectures I deliver are usually fun and informative. I take on the role of a stand-up comedienne.

That particular day, we had had over two hundred people jamming the auditorium. Typically, we choose a half-dozen couples at random and have a little fun with them. This day I was in rare form, and the audience was with me.

If I see something ominous through my handwriting analysis, I play it down. I have always believed that you should make the deposit before the withdrawal.

Amanda and Paul were engaged to be married shortly. They were traveling with their parents on this cruise, and they happened to be one of the couples I had selected for handwriting analyses.

Their future, they told me, depended on my input—not only for their lifetime commitment but for a "dream" house they were preparing to build, which would accentuate their individual lifestyle.

I immediately spotted something wrong. Amanda's writing was very large and covered the whole page. The way you fill your piece of paper is the way you fill your space in life. Her *t* bars were high, way past her *t*'s and flying across the page. She was a romantic—a dreamer with castles floating in the clouds. There weren't enough hours in the day for Amanda. She had a tremendous amount of scattered energy.

Paul's writing, on the other hand, was tiny, clear, and to the point, which indicated to me that he was very focused, detail-oriented, and meticulous. Every *i* dot was placed directly over the *i* and every *t* bar was in the center of the *t*.

It was obvious that Amanda needed people and Paul needed his private space, even though he enjoyed being with close friends.

Should I indicate that they may not be compatible, or should I turn romantic and tell them never mind the differences—that opposites in most cases attract each other?

Did I do the right thing? Handwriting analysis is not the answer to all problems. It is merely another technique for assessing whether there are problems. I took the side of the romanticist. I told them that they were made for each other: to go for it and build their dream house together.

They could be a good balance for each other, I felt. Amanda would bring excitement and spontaneity to Paul. Paul would keep Amanda well grounded and maintain the necessary stability.

I have had the opportunity of analyzing thousands of handwritings over a period of twenty years, but when I met Paul and Amanda, I felt a closeness and believed our paths would cross again one day.

The months flew by, and I was very curious as to how that love match turned out. I needn't have been concerned. My turning and tossing proved to be for naught. I received a letter (would you believe it was postmarked Sugar Notch, Pennsylvania?) from Amanda and Paul with a picture of their dream house. They looked extremely happy, and so did their newest addition, a baby girl they named Alice Stefanie Wilson—A.S.W. happen to be my initials.

ALICE STERN WEISER

> *"Stress is when your mouth says yes
> and your gut says no."*
> —Author unknown

LEADING FROM THE HEART

As a new businesswoman, with a fresh M.B.A. at the age of twenty-eight, I thought I knew it all! I moved up quickly in my first position with a major corporation and soon found myself managing six hundred–plus women.

I had learned well how to manage the numbers, increasing our profits and finding new market niches. What I had not learned in business school was the human element—how to be a leader of people, not just a "manager."

A key aspect of my role was to give speeches to our staff at our semiannual meetings. Public speaking terrified me, as I had no idea what I could say that would be of interest to anyone. And some four hundred associates attended at these meetings—a daunting number.

My boss, a middle-aged gentleman, coached me to give updates on the business. To lessen the damage to my psyche, I would prepare and rehearse my speeches. I mastered the numbers—our profitability, our business direction, our venturing into new markets.

At one of these meetings, I had prepared my speech, done the requisite rehearsal in front of my mirror, and perfected my index cards for prompting. I was ready—or so I thought.

I stepped up to the podium and began my speech. People began to drift away. I heard an inner voice tell me, "They hate this! They're all wondering when it will be over and lunch will be served! Why do you always give these speeches, when you know they don't work?"

I looked up from my notes to check on the women in the first few rows. Sure enough, they seemed pulseless! I stopped and really looked at them (at least the few I dared to establish eye contact with). I made a quick decision. Loudly crumpling my speech into a big wad, I threw it over my shoulder. "Aw, the heck with this!" I stunned the audience and myself.

Having done that—quite dramatically, I might add—I looked out at the audience again. What was I going to say now? I still had fifteen minutes left for my presentation! After a few anxious moments, I said, "Let's talk about how we are doing and what's next. We are having a fantastic year, and we should be celebrating!"

I went on to talk about all our achievements, what I dreamed of for our organization, and how, together, we could do anything! The "speech" was a big hit! Instead of talking at them, I talked with them.

That day was most memorable for me. I learned that to succeed with people—especially women—you have to relate on a human level. What you *know* isn't as important as establishing trust and letting others know who you are. I needed to give them insight into who *I* was, what *I* valued, and how much *I* cared before I could gain their commitment and enthusiasm. I now call it "leading from the heart."

A few years later, I spoke again to this same group. Having grown significantly on the job, I had decided to move on to new challenges. The person I had been grooming was ready to take over my position, and I was to introduce her.

As I finished my remarks, the group stood up, one by one. I received my first standing ovation! I realized then how much my associates had taught me about leadership. A true leader communicates with people. A true leader allows others to lead, empowers others for success, and leads from the heart.

I also learned how amazing it is when people are truly on "speaking terms" with one another—whether with an audience of four hundred or with a single friend.

Holly Esparza

"The naked truth is always better than the best-dressed lie."
—Ann Landers

MY SAILOR MAN

Both of us between husbands and feeling carefree, a friend and I ventured to a dance club playing sixties rock 'n' roll music one night in the early eighties.

We stood in the back, watching the theatrics of both dancers and band. Absorbed in the atmosphere, I hadn't noticed the young man standing next to me until he asked for a dance.

His name was Terry, and he served as a first mate on a dredge ship currently in dry dock on the banks of the Columbia River. A merchant marine, he enjoyed the luxury of working one week on and one week off. As we talked, I recognized a spiritual kinship. On his reading list were *The Road Less Traveled* by M. Scott Peck and *Illusions* by Richard Bach. All evening we discussed the power of positive thought, the creative potential everyone possesses, the oneness of humanity—not the usual bar conversation. But we both communicated that neither of us wanted a committed relationship, just companionship. We both lied.

I admired his appearance—tall, six feet three, great physique, dark, thick hair, dark-brown almond-shaped eyes, and an exotic aura, the result of his Indonesian and Dutch heritage. I imagined him posing for the pages of some studly magazine, instead of holding me in his arms on the dance floor. That evening, I left the club enamored.

The following day he met my three children. I warmed at his instant rapport with them. His potential as a partner increased moment by moment. Already I'd formed a list of positive attributes beyond the obvious physical ones—like the mutual fondness between him and my children, and his embrace of a similar spiritual philosophy. Over the years, I came to discover a deeply compassionate soul, an attentive listener, a wise human being. The measure of his thoughtfulness and kindness caught me off guard. When my children's birthdays came around, he offered gifts to both them and me. "It's a big day for you too," Terry said. "This is the anniversary of the day you labored them into life." I throve on his unconditional love of me.

In the four years we dated, I kept watching for the emergence of his dark side. The only annoying thing I ever came up with was that he held his face too close to his plate when he ate—a ship-born habit. Without a good handle on his "grub," his plate might end up in shipmate's lap, especially on the open seas. Wasn't much of a defect, but it was all that surfaced.

We harbored a dinosaur in the living room, however, an irreconcilable difference, which we both ignored. Terry was eleven years younger than I. At his age, I'd married, borne three children, owned a home, and struggled through a divorce. I'd already lived a life he had yet to experience. Terry never kept his love of children a secret, or his desire for parenthood. He became a volunteer in the Children's Celebration at our church, joined a Big Brother program, and visited his home in North Carolina, as much to play with his nieces and nephews as to see the rest of his family. I'd made it perfectly clear that there'd be no more babies for me. The years of raising three children alone convinced me.

Neither of us wanted to address the dinosaur; we tiptoed around the monster. After all, we fit together, were comfortable, happy, and in love. But always, in the back of my mind, I couldn't bear the thought of his relinquishing parenthood to remain with me. On Saint Patrick's Day, 1985, while both of us sat crying into green beers at Paddy's Bar, I said goodbye. We agreed to continue supporting each other emotionally until we discovered our perfect mates. His arrived sooner than mine. Within a year, he met Rita, a young Irish student majoring in early childhood education. A suitable match. Too distraught to attend the wedding, I sent my love and then hopped on a plane for San Francisco to visit my daughter.

After he married, I stumbled in and out of meaningless relationships. Occasionally, I'd see him and Rita at church, but I tried to avoid them. One look at my face, and Rita would know that I still loved her husband. I'd spare them that. True relationships are eternal, I told myself. I'll keep his memory close to my heart. Maybe we'll meet again in the afterlife.

Sundays, it was my job at church to attempt to regulate the noise during the minister's meditation time by bouncing noisy children with their parents into the family room. One Sunday, hearing a whimpering child in front of me, I placed my hand on the father's shoulder. Terry's eyes looked up. Neither of us spoke. Slowly he rose to face me, then he held out his arms, offering me his baby girl. Except for her blond hair, she epitomized Terry. I held her close to my heart, cradling and comforting her. "You could have been mine," I whispered in her ear. "You could have been mine." Tears streamed from my eyes, dampening her blanket. When Terry and Rita rose for the group song, I returned their child. In the darkened church, I felt certain my tear-smudged makeup wouldn't give me away. Terry's soft eyes held mine for a long moment. We remained silent. Then he turned his attention back to his family and to the service. Quietly I slipped out of the room to weep over this final chapter in our love story.

Within a few more years, I'd meet and marry my life partner. But that day, the radiance in Terry's face as he offered me his child assured me that I'd made the right choice. I could only thank God for teaching me the truth about unconditional love. Sometimes it's best to love from a distance. . . . Other times, it means letting go.

LINDA ROSS SWANSON

*"To love what you do and feel that it matters—
how could anything be more fun?"*
—Katharine Graham

FEEDBACK IS A GIFT

My training work takes me into a wide range of corporate settings, from old-line financial institutions to funky communications firms. And I observe in my workshops a wide range of ways in which we make our professional lives harder on ourselves than we need to.

One technology company I consulted with operated in a highly competitive market where speed and product integrity were the keys to success. They were under tremendous pressure, both internally and from clients; and the employees needed each other's help and feedback in order to produce. Unfortunately, the prevailing atmosphere of fear, anger, and general paranoia made it hard to give and harder to get.

And now ten participants were gathered around the conference table for a session on "Giving and Receiving Feedback."

I had prepared my usual snappy two hours' worth of exercises, ideas, small-group breakout sessions, flip-chart lists, etc. My professional style is to be highly prepared, "buttoned up," and firmly in control.

We started with eliciting people's feelings about how feedback was or was not working in their environment. The bottom line was it wasn't working. People were upset and bitter about it; and even though each person wanted to be treated better, they had a hard time translating that into how to treat others.

I introduced an exercise I'd read about. Each participant

wrote his or her name at the top of a piece of paper, then the papers were passed around the table, until everyone had written a positive piece of feedback ("Something I like or admire or appreciate or respect or value about what you do") on everyone else's paper.

So far, so good. Papers were returned. And ten people now sat with a piece of paper in front of them, listing nine statements of positive feedback from their colleagues.

I took a deep breath. "Who would like to volunteer to have your paper passed around again? Only this time, the writers will read aloud to you what they wrote—and they can expand on their comment, if they wish. All you need to do is sit, listen, and say thank you. In fact, 'Thank you' is all you may say. Any takers?"

Silence. Chairs tilted back from the table. Eyes were averted. Doodling got intense. Nervous giggling. "Not me." "Nope." "I'm not going first." Blank looks into the mid-distance. The room was stuffed so thickly with tension, it seemed to cut off our air supply.

"Wait a minute, folks," I commented, "This is the good stuff. This is positive feedback, remember? This is what you want to hear."

Finally, a reluctant volunteer tossed her paper into the ring. "OK, let's go." She grimaced, crossing her arms protectively in front of her.

It started haltingly, awkwardly, and gradually it built upon itself. People heard from their peers words of thanks and encouragement and praise, everything from "I appreciate that you always say good morning when I come in" to "I'm amazed at how you manage to come up with off-the-cuff ideas when we're in client meetings."

They began to look at one another, making real eye contact. Readers began to elaborate on their written comments, expanding into longer and longer heartfelt comments. People couldn't wait to volunteer next. A huge void in the room, an emptiness that we had hardly perceived earlier and had barely realized needed filling, slowly began to fill with goodwill. And as that emptiness that we hadn't even recognized (it was just "corporate culture," "the way things were") began to change, body language changed. Breathing got deeper. The energy in the room shifted. It got slower, broader, more inclusive, and flowed generously out to others instead of being hoarded tightly inside.

I watched, spellbound, the faces of the givers of this feedback and those receiving it. People were glowing. And I, too, was moved by the immense shift in energy. I left center stage and sat down, quietly, to the side. I stopped directing. I put away my watch. I lowered my voice. I understood I was witnessing something extraordinary, and the rest of the planned workshop certainly wasn't going to continue according to my schedule—what was happening in front of me was far too important.

This day had created its own rhythm. The tremendous collective need we all have to be recognized and appreciated for our work had taken hold, and the participants were basking in words of acceptance.

What a powerful lesson we learned! Our personal needs as individuals can be honored in professional settings in a way that will make us that much more empowered to do the job. I've never met anyone yet who didn't work better when she or he felt better.

Or as Ray, one of the participants, said to me a few days later: "I always thought feedback was something to fear—no one ever seems to have anything good to say around here. So I guess I made it pretty hard on anyone who tried to talk to me. I sort of shut myself off from that stuff, and I probably wasn't the easiest guy to work with. But I can't tell you how surprised I was to hear my co-workers had noticed my work and really respected my contributions. That just blew me away. In fact, I'm taking a whole new approach—now I think feedback is a gift."

I couldn't have said it any better myself.

DIANE RIPSTEIN

RHYMES AND REASONS

As I sang to my newborn son, I contemplated my decision. The tune soothed my baby and me.

When I think about Patrick, my firstborn, I remember how difficult those first few months were. Whenever he got restless, I'd draw from my teaching days and sing a rhyme or two.

Patrick's first cry had been in late August—and so was the first day of school for my former students. I missed the cheerful faces of the schoolchildren and the musty smell of a closed-up classroom. Had I made the right decision? Should I have continued teaching after having a baby? Would I lose contact with my teaching peers and fade into lost volumes of aging yearbooks?

As conflicted as I was, I knew seeing my young baby mature into a toddler and a little boy was something I did not want to miss. On snowy mornings past, I'd be scraping my windshield before work. Now I was cuddling my son under warm blankets and watching the snow fall. An afternoon at the museum, a visit to the library story hour, or a walk around the block was very special for both of us.

While most of my focus was on mother-child activities, I also found time to sew and read, luxuries that were virtually nonexistent before. I enjoyed making Patrick's pumpkin costume for Halloween and felt proud of his Christmas stocking, with the sequins I had worked so hard to apply, hanging on the fireplace mantel.

Unfortunately, we at-home moms are many times misunderstood. I am asked, "Why are you wasting your life and career staying at home?"

My reply is simple. "I can always go back to teaching, but never to those wonderful days of motherhood." What a sad commentary on society when the most important job in the world must be defended.

It has been six years since I made this decision. It is just as special to see two more stockings above our fireplace (yes, with sequins too!) and the costume gallery I have created since that first October.

I walked near my sons' room last night and listened to Anthony corral his imaginary puppies and Dominic wail for attention. I started to enter and comfort my little one, only to be pleasantly surprised by my oldest son singing those same rhymes from my teaching days to calm his littlest brother.

As I leaned against the door, a new song filled my heart. It was then I realized I hadn't given up teaching at all!

Antionette Vigliaturo Ishmael

> *"In search of my mother's garden,*
> *I found my own."*
> —Alice Walker

IT'S ALL IN THE FRIJOLES

The last six weeks of my mother's life became an opportunity for me to seek wisdom, to give thanks for all she had given me, and to rectify old hurts.

I was adamant about not leaving any unfinished business between us. I wanted to end our time together on good terms. Why else was I given a warning about Mom's limited time on this planet just days before her terminal diagnosis?

The warning had come in the middle of the night while I was in a twilight dream state. "It's time for me to go... it's time for me to go," she told me. I immediately got up, dressed, and drove to her home, twenty minutes away.

I half expected her to be gone when I arrived, but when I walked quietly into her bedroom, she woke up and asked, "What are you doing here?"

"I dreamed you told me it was time for you to go, and I didn't want you to leave until I told you I love you."

"I love you too, but not at four o'clock in the morning," she replied. That was the first glimpse I got of Mom's wry sense of humor.

Four days later, she collapsed. The doctor told me she was suffering from kidney disease and gave her six weeks to live.

My mother was a physically small woman, five feet tall. Born in Mexico, she had only an eighth-grade education and had made her living as a seamstress. But she was a woman of tremendous character and discipline.

To set a good example, Mom went back to school to achieve her own high school diploma when I was in high school. She worked to improve her English by daily reading the newspaper out loud, and helped friends and relatives as they went through their struggles with the language.

She read biographies and autobiographies written by famous and often self-made men and women, along with fine literature and poetry. She loved to read lessons from the Bible and from *Science and Health with Key to the Scriptures* each morning before going to work. Mom was strong and tough-minded, wise and practical, elegant, refined, and gracious.

One day as she lay in bed a few weeks after the grim medical diagnosis, I asked her what made her so strong. The sun streamed through the French windows of her bedroom as I leaned forward in anticipation of the wisdom I was about to receive, sure it would transform my life.

I had expected to hear her draw from the teachings of Mary Baker Eddy, discoverer and founder of Christian Science, and one of her role models. Or to draw upon an inspirational quote from the Bible.

"Beans! Beans have made me strong." I laughed, but was somewhat disappointed that she didn't leave me with a stronger message.

It wasn't until months after her death, as I was preparing *frijoles de la olla*, and recalled Mom's instructions on how to cook the perfect beans, that I realized the power of her deathbed message to me.

Mom took great care in washing and sorting her beans. After running water over them several times, she would spread them out on a tray or a large dish and then pick out and discard any imperfectly shaped, shriveled, or dark-colored beans. She always eyed them carefully. Each bean for her pot had to be a perfectly flawless pinto. "A bad bean can sour the pot," she would say.

Mom also cautioned me against adding cold water to the cooking pot if the water evaporated below a certain point, or the beans would turn dark and not appear fresh when served. Her beans were not only delicious but pretty to look at.

While I was cooking, I realized what Mom had meant months earlier.

Not only are beans the staple of the Mexican diet and filled with strength-giving iron, but the rigor she applied to eliminating any undesirable beans was the same exacting attention she paid to eliminating character flaws and weaknesses in herself and those around her. The beans were a vivid example of what she had tried to teach me as a young girl.

And so I finally got it. What all that tough love was about. The emphasis upon developing character and self-control. Taking in only the good and rejecting the bad. That day, in the kitchen, I understood why beans made my mother so strong.

YOLANDA NAVA

"Surround yourself with people who respect you and treat you well."
—Claudia Black

SOMETHING TO CHEW ON

Confidence in yourself is like money in the bank. I've heard that eighty-five percent of your success comes from having confidence in yourself. This is one of the key points I teach in success seminars, and one I learned the hard way.

Several years ago, I had a boss who got belligerent every time he had a few drinks at lunch. When he returned to the office from one of those two- or three-hour "business lunches," he'd always pick on somebody. We all dodged when we saw him coming. But one day I didn't duck fast enough, and I became his victim.

He chewed me out loud and long in front of several of my co-workers. (He obviously hadn't heard that it's important to praise in public and criticize in private.) By the time he was through yelling at me, my confidence was down the tubes. And the worst part was that I still had to tape a TV show that afternoon and give a lecture to hundreds of people that night. I had a tough time making it through my appearances. I choked up a few times, remembering the devastating things my boss had said to me earlier.

I'm a tenderhearted person who cries easily, and I cried all night long, humiliated by the verbal lashing that afternoon.

Once the tears dried up, I knew I had to take action to get my confidence back. Lying in bed the next morning, I thought of everything I'd learned about building confidence and self-esteem. Silently I listed all my good qualities, before slipping out of bed to retrieve my "Treasure Box." This special box is filled with notes of appreciation I've received, newspaper clippings about me, honors, and love notes from my husband and my sons. My spirits were buoyed after reading several pieces. Then I developed a plan to turn around the situation with my boss. I noticed my confidence rising already just by my thinking of taking positive action.

"I need to talk with you, please," I said as I walked into my boss's office next day. He looked apprehensive as he motioned me toward the chair in front of his massive desk. The chair was low, to intimidate others. I smiled warmly at him while making a point of sitting as tall and proud as I could.

"I'm sorry I upset you yesterday," I told him, "and there are some facts you haven't heard." Calmly I pointed out the information he was missing, and then I asked, "Now, could you tell me something good about me? After all," I added in jest, "you're the one who hired me, and I wouldn't want you to jeopardize your credibility with the staff!"

He stared at me hard for a few moments, then released his arms from their grip across his chest. He started listing positive things about me—many more than I had expected. I walked out of his office feeling more validated than I had expected. My being proactive was definitely working.

A couple of weeks later, though—right after lunch—the boss's secretary called me on the intercom. "Rita," she said, "he's *really* upset and on his way to chew you out. I know how he demoralizes everyone. Get ready."

My heart sank only momentarily, then I stood up, chuckled to myself, and stepped out into the hallway to wait for him. I had his number! There he came, his temples pulsating, his fists clenched, and his teeth all but bared. He was primed for me with both barrels. I smiled widely and waved real friendly-like, as if to say, *Come on down!* He hesitated as it dawned on him: When he got through chewing me out, I was going to say, "Okay, now say something good about me!" Instantly, he wheeled around and stalked back to his office.

Do we hang around and just let someone chew on us at will? Never. If we can't make a significant difference with that person, it's time to make plans to move on. In my case, however, once I dealt with my emotions, the solution was simple. I asked for what I needed! By doing so, I was able to make a large deposit into my "bank of confidence."

RITA DAVENPORT

VIII
THE ANIMAL CONNECTION

"No animal should ever jump up on the dining room furniture unless absolutely certain that [she] can hold [her] own in the conversation."

—Fran Lebowitz

*"To keep something you must care for it;
more, you must understand what kind of care it requires."*
—Dorothy Parker

ONE SOUL, TWO HALVES

My husband grew up on a farm where his family raised horses and dogs, so he has spent much of his life in the presence of animals. Yet he remarks in reference to Cali and me, "I have never known an animal and a human who were more like two halves of the same soul."

I was a young teacher working in a foreign country and she a two-month-old ball of matted fur when we met. I decided a German shepherd dog would be a good companion for a single female living alone in a remote village. Big and robust by four and a half months, Cali stepped on a scorpion ambling across the porch one night and was quickly reduced to an immobile, lethargic pup. How she managed to live through the incident I do not know; a friend's puppy, two weeks younger, had died from such a bite within two hours.

Cali lived, but she was completely paralyzed. She could not even move her mouth to eat, so I fed her by dripping raw egg down the back of her throat. Her body deteriorated so much so that her coarse hair turned curly from coiling around the bones protruding through her coat. As if that wasn't bad enough, she developed a blood infection and high fever from the wound, so I carried her across the country on rattletrap buses and in my arms to an American vet, who put her on IV fluids for a week and then sent us home, saying there was nothing more to be done. Nonetheless, I collected water at night and submerged her in it during the day to control her fever. And so we lived for over a month: I, at five feet three and one hundred pounds, carrying a forty-pound paralyzed dog across my shoulders everywhere I went, and she defying death.

Having spent so much time carrying her around with me to monitor her health, I felt it was silly to leave her home once she recovered and was able to get around on her own. She hiked with me through the mountains and curled up under a child's desk each day in the rural schools where I taught. She ate her dinner next to me on the dirt floor each night, and when I went to use the "bathroom" behind a tree, she would squat next to me. We were constant companions and best friends, and to this day I can think of nothing we would not do for each other.

Not that I needed proof of this loyalty, but she demonstrated it one night after I'd moved to a house with a bedroom that opened directly onto an enclosed courtyard. The outer double doors were made of two pieces of wood, which were attached to the adobe walls with rusty nails and supported inside by a two-by-four. A strong wind could have knocked down that door; but I was due to return to the States in just a few months and had become somewhat complacent. Besides, I arrogantly assumed I was young and strong and could take care of myself in an emergency.

Cali's growls woke me in the middle of the night as she stood guard over me on top of the bed, facing the door with her teeth bared. I heard footsteps on the concrete patio outside, advancing slowly toward the bedroom door. Never in my twenty-four years had the implications of a sound been clearer to me; never had I been more terrified. While I had rehearsed such a scenario in my head countless times—how I would defend myself with quick kicks to the shin and groin and blows to the bridge of the nose—when the moment to act presented itself, I was immobilized by fear. My body was like lead; I could not even move my arm to reach for the knife I kept hidden under my pillow. I just lay there, unable to breathe, sure I would suffocate before the man outside had a chance to kill me. "Breathe!" I said to myself, and finally managed to suck in a gulp of air. The footsteps echoed closer, and still I could not move.

As he threw his body against the door to break through, Cali leapt from the bed, and their bodies hit those two wooden boards at exactly the same time. Through the cracks in the wood, she clawed at him with her paws and slashed at him with her teeth. Still he persisted. Yet every time he stepped back and flung his body at the door to break it down from the outside, she flung her body at it from the inside and held up that rickety old door. After what seemed like an eternity but could not have been more than twenty seconds, he ran off—as scared of my dog as I had been of him. This time it was she who saved me.

The more time we spent together, the closer we became, until the similarities seemed almost eerie to those who do not trust in the bonds between animals and the humans they love. Whenever I got a cold, so did Cali. When my allergies got bad after I'd returned to the States, Cali developed allergies too, and after a series of tests, it was determined that we are actually allergic to the same foods and pollens. When my allergies improved, so did hers. At my wedding, a large outdoor affair, a friend held Cali on a leash throughout the ceremony. Just as the minister asked, "Do you take this man?" and right before I responded "I do," a long, loud howl echoed from the back of the crowd. It was Cali, most surely saying, "I do too."

Unfortunately, the similarities did not end there. Six months after I was diagnosed with a benign heart murmur, Cali was also diagnosed with a heart murmur. We were driving cross-country on our honeymoon, with Cali in the back seat. She had developed a weepy eye, and I was concerned some road dust was irritating it, so we stopped at a veterinary hospital in Salt Lake City to have it checked. The vet looked at her eyes, then as part of the routine exam put the stethoscope to Cali's chest. His forehead furrowed and he bit his lip as he moved the stethoscope across her body for a full five minutes. Finally, he straightened up and addressed us. "Her eyes are fine," he said, "but she has a serious heart condition." As I held her and cried, we did an immediate ultrasound to confirm his diagnosis: subaortic stenosis. There really was not anything to be done; the cardiac specialist we took her to said he had never heard a worse heart. "If you treat her normally, she has two months to live," he said. "But if you keep her inside at all times, prevent her from running around or exerting any energy, she may have a life span of up to two years."

"I can't do that," I said. "She plays outside every day; we run together all the time. She'd be absolutely miserable locked up inside."

"Then you'll kill her," the vet said.

"But she'll die happy," I retorted. "I know she'd prefer a short, happy life to a long, miserable one." Though devastated at her prognosis, I relished the opportunity to ensure that the end of her life would be as much fun as the beginning had been.

That was well over three years ago. Cali and I walk or jog a couple of miles to the park every day—depending on my level of stamina!—where she plays with a pack of dog friends and swims in the river. She has since traveled back and forth across the country twice more, has hiked the redwood forest, and is so healthy that the only reason we go to the vet anymore is to update her vaccines. Oh, her heart is still in terrible condition. In fact, whenever we do go to the vet, the staff always asks politely if everyone in the office can listen to it. "You'll never hear a heart like this again," they say to one another. The vet admits he has never seen a healthier-looking dog with a worse heart, and adds that there is no medical explanation for her longevity.

I can explain it, though. Cali teaches me every day that there are forces greater than medicine and technology. From the minute she recovered from that scorpion bite, she has repaid my nurturing with unwavering loyalty and friendship. She has been the guardian of not only my physical body but also my soul. In times of loneliness and fear, she has again and again offered herself wholeheartedly and unselfishly to me. Out of love for me, she continues to live.

I am no fool; I know that eventually Cali will die. Nonetheless, I have had the opportunity to share my soul with a wise and generous teacher. When I needed it most, God sent me an angel disguised in fur to remind me of the power of love.

Ellen Urbani Hiltebrand

KEEPING THE HIGH WATCH

*A*lmost home, fifteen minutes ahead of schedule. I had just enough time to change clothes before jumping back into the car for a forty-five-mile commute to meet a real estate agent who was showing me a property in my soon-to-be "new neighborhood." A stoplight! Damn it—the longest light in the area.

While waiting for the light to change, I caught a glimpse of a rather large bird, flying low. A very small bird appeared to be nipping at the large bird's tail, as if in attack. But after watching awhile, I realized that the larger bird was the mother, that the small bird must be taking its fledgling flight. Suddenly the baby bird lost altitude and fluttered erratically, obviously unable to stay aloft. The mother swooped down and lifted the baby on her back into the still, clear-blue sky, and then pulled away again. Unsteadily, the baby regained its flying ability, and the mother remained only inches away. Slowly the mother moved a few feet to the side, and then a few feet below. Baby was doing fine.

Tooting horns at the signal change reminded me that others needed to move their cars for destinations unknown. I drove slowly, observing my birds. Watching this momentous occasion for baby and the loving, protective measures by mom had become more important than any scheduled appointment. So I would delay my meeting fifteen more minutes. This was life!

I thought back to when my baby took her first steps. First I held her hand and then, ever so gently, I released it, but keeping my hands close enough to catch her if necessary. My eyes swelled with tears. I felt such love for a mother who nurtured and was now helping to release her young to follow the path of life. My own daughter had had a baby nine months earlier and was experiencing motherhood for the first time.

We release our young so many times, in so many ways. Their first steps, their first days at school, their first dates, going away to college, and of course marriage. But we never release them from our hearts.

Mom and baby bird were soaring freely as I approached my garage. No time to spare now—I raced to the door. The phone began to ring. Oh, let the machine answer it, was my first thought, but I felt compelled to answer. Another five minutes down the drain, I thought.

My daughter was calling from her home, fifteen hundred miles away, with news that her son, my grandson, had taken his first steps minutes before. I began to cry. I believed that I had been there in some beautiful, unexplainable way. God had shared the moment with me.

I called my real estate agent and had her rearrange the appointment for a few hours later that day. I went for a walk on the beach and sat awhile, just looking out over this beautiful world. Taking a deep breath, I looked up. Birds soared overhead. And my grandson had started his own journey through life. Carefully, I hope—one baby step at a time.

EILEEN DAVIS

> *"Dogs' lives are too short. Their only fault, really."*
> —Agnes Sligh Turnbull

DAZY JOY

She had been failing for almost a year when she stopped eating. The next day, she took no water. Being human, I wanted her to live. Using the turkey baster, I tried to drip liquids down her throat, but she turned her head away. "Enough," she seemed to say with her eyes. "It's time for me to die."

With that she crawled into my lap and allowed me to rock her slowly back and forth. Hours we spent together that day, her thin shepherd body draped over my arms, my face against her neck, memories swirling in my head.

I thought about the day we first met. Apparently the school stray, a beggar and a botherer of students and faculty alike, she was tied to a bench, awaiting the arrival of the dogcatcher, when I breezed into the university office. We looked into each other's eyes, and our souls met. I untied her, carried her to my office, and fed the starving young animal. In no time, she was in the back seat of my car, heading to her new home.

My husband and I named her Dazy Joy, and she became our constant companion and most devoted friend. She went everywhere with us: vacations, day trips, family dinners, and holidays. She became the matriarch of the family, frequently barking out instructions as if she could talk.

Over the next many years, Dazy Joy served as overseer to the dozens of rescued animals who came and went at our home. A firm disciplinarian, she was also tolerant of the newcomers. Yet in spite of the many pets and people who occupied her space over the years, she never relinquished her role as guardian over us, the animals, and the house.

She could always read my mind.

So on that final day, sensing I'd reached a restful place in my mindful reverie, she slipped out of my arms and stood solidly on the floor. In tears, I watched Dazy Joy amble her tired, weak body from room to room in the house. No door was left unnudged as she entered and paused in each space to look around. Her purpose seemed twofold. Using every bit of the strength she had left, she was saying goodbye. And before letting go of her role as guardian over me, Dazy Joy needed to check one last time to make sure all would be well in my world. Satisfied, she walked to the front door and beckoned for me to follow her.

That day, sixteen and a half years after our first meeting, we made the journey back to the fate from which I had once saved her. I held her close as she willingly accepted the medicine. Eight years later, I still hold her close. A framed picture of her on my nightstand is my constant reminder.

CINDY POTTER

"Dogs will come when called.
Cats will take a message and get back to you."
—Missy Dizick and Mary Bly

OSCAR

We first met Sylvester when he emerged from the shrubbery in our front yard. He was timid but hungry, and his plaintive "meooww" was obviously a request for food. My husband, Rocky, and I began to bring him scraps of food each afternoon, and he came to expect them, showing up at the same time each day. He was a stray one—a tomcat who lived in the woods, and we began to feel responsible for this independent little spirit. But we weren't ready to call him "our cat" just yet. We named him Sylvester because he looked just like the cartoon character, with the same markings and tufts of fur on his cheeks. You could almost hear him say, "Thufferin' thuccotath!"

I realized it was high time for inoculations and neutering after he'd had a run-in with a family of raccoons. They beat him up good and tore big patches of fur off his hide. So I made the appointment with the veterinarian for the following week. We decided he had "adopted" us and he was now ours. But it wasn't to be. A couple of days later, I found Sylvester on the back porch, lying very still. I rushed him to the vet, where he died that night.

It was a sad day for Rocky and me.

"If only we'd gotten his shots sooner, if only we'd taken better care of him," we lamented. In the next few days, for some reason the name Oscar kept popping up in my head. I mentioned it to my husband, and we agreed to name our next cat Oscar—but only when we were ready for one.

A week or so later, my mother called and said she had a cat for me. I told her I wasn't over Sylvester yet, and besides, I thought I'd wait awhile. But my mother was unusually insistent.

"This cat needs a home or he'll be taken to the Humane Society!"

She said her friend Bernie was feeding the cat. It had been abandoned at her apartment, where she could not have a pet.

"I really appreciate your intentions, Mom, but no, thanks. Does the cat have a name?"

"Yes," she said. "Bernie calls him Oscar."

Chills traveled down my spine. I knew this was my cat! When I went to pick him up, I fell in love immediately. This little fellow had a big gray splotch on his nose. He looked me in the eye and came right up to me, as if to say, "It's about time you got here."

Oscar is still with us. He must have been a very successful stray, because when we first got him, he was a little chubby. We put him on low-fat cat food, got his shots, and had him "fixed."

He is, as Bernie put it, "A very fine kitty indeed." We call him a dozen different variations of his original name—Osca-furball, Oscalario, Oscabidilly-oskies—to fit his moods.

I feel as though this cat came my way for a reason. Oscar has given me the gift of a second chance at "motherhood." The fact that I knew his name before I even knew of him confirms my belief in what many other cat lovers know—that I didn't find my cat; he found me.

CINDY HANSON

LOOK-ALIKE LUCYS

Soft and fuzzy, with slightly worn light-brown fur, the little bear looks as though she has been hugged a lot. Her eyes are shiny black and her nose is an upside-down triangle made of yarn. I am constantly brushing the fur out of her eyes, so she can see better.

When I first saw my Lucy, she was sitting in a store window, tucked in with a hundred other teddy bears. But she stood out like she was the only one. She looked just like my daughter's bear. As we stared at each other through the window, my eyes filled with tears. Knowing she would be coming home with me, and that she represented much more than a stuffed bear, I took a few moments to compose myself before going into the store to purchase her.

"Bears don't like bags," I said as the clerk handed me the change. "I'll carry her." Lucy felt comfortable under my arm, as if she belonged there. A gentle stirring in my heart, and a measure of the peace I had been seeking settled in.

My soft bear lay snuggled under the covers between us that night as my husband and I talked quietly about the other Lucy. Our daughter Janice had loved the life into her Lucy, until even we thought it was real. Jan would tell us about the bear's daily adventures, weaving elaborate tales of mischief and fun. Laughing, she blamed Lucy for the crumbs on her sheets, saying the little bear sneaked cookies into her bed. In later years, Lucy took rides in Janice's car, secure in a seat belt until a cute guy pulled up next to them. Then the two of them would wave madly, getting the boy's attention and a big smile.

Janice often moved bears from my collection to her room down the hall. Baby Bear was her favorite. Investigating, I would find the two bears, Baby Bear and Lucy, keeping company in the old wooden rocker, "sharing stories and waiting for tea," Janice would tell me with a straight face.

Lucy became her confidante, listening attentively to endless chatter about school and horses and boyfriends. Once in a while, tears of a young girl's frustration and disappointment matted the fluffy fur. The little bear gave quiet, unconditional love, and Jan loved her back.

The games we played with the bears added humor and lightness to the sometimes difficult teenage years, when independence was important to her and guidance was important to me.

We were the best of friends and still playing bear games when Janice died suddenly, at the age of twenty-two. Her Lucy rests with her, and I picture the two of them laughing and scheming as they continue their adventures together.

I slept with my Lucy for several years after Janice's death. The wise little bear seemed to listen with all her heart when I talked of happy memories, or whispered how much I missed the fun and laughter Janice and I shared. Sometimes, when the grief was overwhelming, she caught the tears of sadness. Always, she felt warm and comforting to hold. She gave me unconditional love, and I loved her back.

Healing comes with time, and I no longer need to sleep with my soft brown confidante. These days, Lucy nestles close to Baby Bear in the old rocking chair and listens to my morning chatter.

I tell her about our four beautiful grandsons and the funny things they say and do. I talk about dinners and hikes with old friends, and describe the new friends I have made. I tell her that I love my art classes and that I will graduate from college soon. Her little mouth is buried in matted fur, but I know she is smiling. I know that Janice and her Lucy are smiling too. And I know that our Lucys are connected to each other, just as Janice and I are connected—through pure love.

SUSAN MILES

A FLUTTER OF
BUTTERFLY WINGS

Mom always told me, "You will try to deny it and you will try to resist it, but you cannot help what you feel."

This thought was going through my head the first time I met Nick. It was not a clap of thunder or an explosion of any sort, but rather like a whispering flutter of butterfly wings in my stomach, a loud beating of my heart . . . bup-bup, bup-bup, bup-bup . . . and my pulse throbbing in my ears.

I waited for the alarm bells to go off in my head. I wanted Nick to grab hold of me and kiss me hard so that those bells would go off, stopping me in my tracks. When the warning bells finally came, I told myself, "Look at your finger! You're practically married to another man!" But every time those bells sounded, I ignored them, because it hurt too much to think that I wasn't in love with the man I was supposed to marry.

I waited for the feelings I had for Nick to go away. I wanted them to go away. It wasn't right to feel this way about another man. But as the days turned into weeks, the weeks into months, I found myself drawn deeper into his world.

The light, male musky scent of him touched my nostrils before he was even in sight. His laughter, deep and thorough, made me smile in response. The feel of his eyes on my back caused me to turn automatically to find him watching me, waiting for me. I could not help wanting him. It was a force I had no control over. Like gravity, it pulled me in.

One day he was sitting at his desk, concentrating—hand in his hair, a frown creasing his brow. I noticed the straight lines of his back and the veins that ran down his arm as he worked. I felt a strange sense of something . . . something akin to pride. Then, before my eyes, I saw him as he would be in fifty years.

His dark hair now gray, the lines of laughter embedded in the skin around his eyes, and the once-straight back slightly stooped with age. The stirring sensation of butterfly wings in my stomach returned with force. That was when I was certain I loved him. I took a deep breath and smiled, finally at peace with myself.

I left my boyfriend and followed my heart. It led me straight into Nick's arms, where I have been ever since. We are married now, and it has been five years since I first felt those butterfly wings fluttering. They are not there every day, nor every time I look at him. But I have found that when I feel I love him the least, they flutter the hardest, and in the times when I love him most, I don't feel or hear them at all. They are simply there as a reminder—from my heart—telling me that I made the right choice.

Lon My Lam

*"When you feel really lousy,
puppy therapy is indicated."*
—Sara Paretsky

A GIFT OF LOVE

Love came bounding into my life on four legs just when I needed it most. Auric—the Latin name for gold—was a golden retriever, with a special capacity for love. He looked and acted like a normal pup, but as he grew, his special qualities became more apparent.

His first year with me was the hardest I've ever known. Not only did my marriage end with a sad betrayal, but I was being stalked by a mentally unstable man. I work as a morning radio personality, and this fan had become obsessed with me after hearing my voice. A restraining order, routine police patrols by my house, and a special alarm system did little to ease my fears. Auric became what little security I had. He stood by me as I peeked out the windows, checking for any signs of my unwanted suitor. At times, he'd check out the house for me, running from room to room as if to show me that nobody was there.

Many nights I'd curl up on the rug in front of the fireplace and fall into a restless sleep. I'd wake up to find Auric lying nearby, watching over me. Some nights, when sleep never came at all, I'd sit alone, crying, trying to rid myself of the pain and fear aching in my heart. Auric never left my side. He'd sit with his head on my knee for hours, offering what comfort he could. And, like any good friend, he knew when I'd wallowed long enough in self-pity. He'd growl and bark—rear end wagging in the air, chin on the floor, a favorite toy stuffed in his mouth—urging me to snap out of it and play. The silliness of his mood would build until I'd agree to a game of fetch or keep-away. He'd have me tearing through the house after him in fits of laughter.

Fortunately, things improved dramatically in our second year together. The "stalker" had been placed on probation, under strictly monitored supervision, and I finally felt free to return to the world of the living.

Auric and I ran the wooded trails near our home, played games in the park, and spent hours fly fishing along a mountain river. He instinctively knew not to bother the wildlife we encountered there. Considering the retriever blood that pulsed through his veins, I regarded this behavior as not only unusual but remarkable.

One bleak winter day near the beginning of his third year, I lost him. I'd lain down for a nap, and I woke to find him gone. He normally sat in the front yard each afternoon, to watch the kids walk home from school. I checked there first, finding no sign of him. Frantic trips around the neighborhood failed to reveal his whereabouts.

I spent weeks tacking up flyers, knocking on doors, and making trips to the shelter. Finally, a worker there took me aside to gently help me face reality. My special dog would not likely be coming home. This kind man explained that someone had probably found or taken Auric and decided to keep him. Privately, I pored through old photos, remembering him. Family and friends listened sympathetically as I choked out my favorite Auric stories. Some of them even shared their own stories with me.

Several months passed, and one Sunday morning I spotted an ad in the newspaper. A family needed to find a home for their two-and-a-half-year-old golden retriever. I drove to the address, secretly expecting to see my long-lost friend bound toward me in fond remembrance. Soul pals, together again! Sad, silly me. Instead I found a shy, sweet lad with quiet manners and an insatiable appetite for a game of fetch. I sank into a lawn chair, elbows on my knees, chin in my hands, and watched.

This dog didn't have the stocky good looks of my old friend. No sign of any uncanny perception visible in his brown eyes, either. The only thing he seemed interested in was a stick being tossed back and forth across the yard. Depression settled over me like a chilly fog. After a few minutes, my sadness gave way to feelings of guilt and worry. What would become of this unwanted dog if I didn't offer him a place to live?

I drove back home with Sam riding in the back of the car, all his worldly possessions in tow; a chipped plastic bowl and a tattered leash. I glanced at him in the rearview mirror. His eyes darted furtively from the back of my head to the rapidly passing landscape beyond the car window. He looked insecure and in desperate need of a friend. Someone with enough time for taking walks and trips to the river and playing games of fetch. I suddenly remembered Auric, and I smiled at the lesson he had taught me about the magic of unconditional love. As I caught another glimpse of Sam, I decided right then and there to open up my heart and give my new pup a chance.

DEBB JANES

IX
ACTS OF KINDNESS

"Too much of a good thing is wonderful."

MAE WEST

THE MEMORY JAR

As Mother's Day approached, I asked myself, "What does Mom *really* want for a gift?" She didn't need another knickknack, I don't know her style or size in clothes anymore, and I used up all my good gift ideas last year (I gave her a fruitcake). I was stumped.

Then it hit me. What she really wants to know is that she made a difference in my life. For many of us, our parents worked hard and sacrificed. Some even gave up their dreams so we could have ours. All they really want is some feedback that their efforts worked! So to say thanks, I made my mother a Memory Jar.

I bought a cut-glass jar with a lid. Then, on one hundred little pieces of paper, I wrote down memories like:

- *I remember our talk the night before I got married.*
- *I remember calling you from the hospital and telling you your first grandchild had been born.*

I set the wrapped cut-glass jar on Mom's coffee table. She edged her way along to the center of the sofa, sat down, and pulled the gift to her lap.

Mom wasn't sure what it was when she saw the label: "The Memory Jar." Noticing her inquisitive look and the arch in her eyebrow, I instructed Mom to take the lid off the jar, reach in, and select a memory.

"Oh," she said. "This is like that old TV show *This Is Your Life!*"

"Kind of," I replied, my voice already trembling. "Except it's really about your life and mine together."

Tears sprang up immediately in her eyes as she read her first memory:

- *I remember you giving me my first bicycle—shiny blue and just my size.*

Mom reached for another slip of paper, and I said, "Wait! You only want to pull one memory out each day and savor it." Finding the memories too irresistible, she laughed, waved me off, and reached into the jar. Mom wanted more memories now!

- *I remember how scared I was (at age nine) when you went to the hospital for surgery.*
- *I remember how I loved to watch you get ready to go out dancing on Saturday night. I knew my mom was the most beautiful mother in the world!*
- *I remember how smart you were raising six kids.*
- *I remember waking up Christmas morning and unwrapping the doll I'd prayed would be under the tree.*
- *I remember saving half the money to buy go-go boots, and the other half you added.*

Mom looked up at me, laughing and crying at once. She whispered, "You've just created a new memory for me. I will always remember this Mother's Day."

I became excited, thinking about the possibility of adding precious memories to the jar from now on. I even felt a twinge of sweet pressure to be sure and create more momentous times to share—especially when Mom read the last memory some time later, looked up at me half-jokingly, and said, "Got any more?"

Mary LoVerde

ROAD WARRIORS

My mother always told me, "Never judge a book by its cover," and as a young girl growing up in the sixties, I tried very hard to follow that sage advice. It was easy back then; I lacked the wisdom and experience to understand that sometimes the cover of a book spoke volumes, that it would tell you everything you needed to know without your ever having to crack the binding. As an adult, I learned that one must trust first impressions, for often they are far more accurate than studied opinion.

One dark night about ten years ago, after a long day of frustrating meetings during which every design I showed my client was critically shredded on the spot, I was driving home on the Massachusetts Turnpike, making the two-hour trip from Springfield to Boston. I was tired and cranky, eager to get home to the comfort of my family. I had stomped out of my last meeting without even bothering to make a pit stop before the drive, and my full bladder was terrorizing me. I comforted myself with the thought that at that late hour there wouldn't be any waiting lines outside the ladies' room at the rest area. It always makes me crazy to see the men waltz right in, while I stand outside fidgeting and twitching, trying to stall off the inevitable.

Pulling off the highway and into the rest area parking lot, I found myself in a forest of huge trucks, grimy gray giants in never-ending rows. I got out of the car and locked it and made my way to the head of the row. As I walked, I saw a man emerging from between two trucks a few rows down. I strained to see him through the darkness, and my first impression was that he blended into the velvety night; in black pants and T-shirt, boots and a cowboy hat, he was just another form of darkness. I began to feel a bit nervous.

He roughly paralleled me as we both made our way through the parking lot, and as he edged closer to me, I could see a greasy blond ponytail hanging down, bouncing off his back as he quickened his pace. I wondered why he was quickening; maybe he had to pee too. But he was looking at me, his expression far too interested for my liking. I saw a cigarette pack rolled into one of his sleeves, a tattoo on his upper arm.

I hurried, leaning into the cool evening breeze. The sound of cars and trucks whizzing by on the turnpike could not overshadow his footsteps, which were faster than my own. He appeared to be younger than I, and for the first time in my life, I felt the fear of a woman growing older, the vulnerability of knowing without doubt that I was slower, weaker, and more frightened than my unwanted "traveling companion."

We drew steadily closer to the building that housed the rest rooms, my salvation, but every time I stepped up my pace, he did so as well. Feeling my heart pound, I looked quickly through the lobby window to see if there was anyone nearby, anyone who would notice and respond if I hurled my purse through the glass door, as I was now contemplating doing. But no one was there; where, I wondered, were the owners of all those trucks? Not where I needed them to be, obviously.

It was ten feet to the door, then five, then three, and then a hand reached out, and I saw it in front of me, and the acid remnants of my last cup of coffee spilled into my gorge. Speech deserted me; I wanted to scream, but nothing would come out. I was completely spitless, dry and pitiable and, I was certain, about to be ravished.

And then the hand settled on the door handle and pulled outward, and the door opened before me as if I were royalty. I stopped and turned slowly, and I stared in shocked relief at my unlikely knight. He stood there, a man I had taken to be a menace, with a cherubic smile on his face. With his other hand, he reached up and removed his hat and in a gentlemanly gesture, swept it down to his chest. "Evenin', ma'am," he said through a gap in his front teeth.

He was so young, just a boy, but oh, what a good boy! A

blossoming man, out on one of his first jobs, pleased with himself and liking the world. I wanted nothing other than to call his mother and tell her what a good job she'd done raising her son. But somehow I think she already knew.

ANN BENSON

*"What would you do
if you knew you could not fail?"*
—Author unknown

FOR THE LOVE OF STUDENTS

It was never quiet at our house. I was born to a college professor father. No student escaped either his compassion when appropriate or his fury at a mediocre performance. His classes were always jammed to overflowing with students of all descriptions and mind-sets. His teaching load exceeded that of any other faculty member, even though his subject was neither particularly popular nor "easy."

And when the students were not in his classroom, they were at our home. Talking and laughing in the house, playing badminton and croquet in our large yard, cooking hamburgers on our backyard grill, sharing—hesitantly and shyly at first, but then with the growing confidence that comes with acceptance and respect—their dreams, their plans for the future, their growing awareness of who they were, what they had to offer, and how they planned to pursue it all.

My dad fed them in the classrooms, and my mother fed them around our table with her own brand of love—bountiful Southern cooking. She had a keen sense of when to be spartan and when to pour out lavishness on others from her own alabaster jar.

We didn't have much money, so my mother had carefully saved all the unspoken-for coins she could stash away. I remember the day when we got the coins out, counted them, and went all the way to Raleigh to buy her dream tablecloth. It was white, beautiful, and pure linen.

From that day on, the Tablecloth was always on our big dining room table. At the end of every day, with good smells filling our house, my mom would make her way through our house and yard, inviting those students who had never had dinner with us before to join our family around the table: a special place where we laughed, poked fun, examined issues, made resolves, and set goals.

At the end of the meal, Mother would hand each student a pencil with a very dull point, and she would say, "Sign your name to our tablecloth, and sometime tomorrow I will take my white linen thread and embroider your name on our cloth."

I remember my dad looking each student directly in the eye and saying, "We want your name on the cloth because the day is going to come when we will be able to say that *you* ate dinner with us when you were just a student."

Every time I look at the Tablecloth, which is now mine, I see the embroidered names of governors, I see Arnold Palmer's name and the names of people who have made a strong mark in our world in medicine, law, and the ministry. I wonder how many of those students whose names cover the cloth succeeded simply because an old professor and his love-filled wife gave them the gift of encouragement.

Emory Austin

LOVE NOTES

One sunny afternoon in May, when pink azalea, purple wisteria, and white dogwood painted our backyard in vibrant colors any child would love, my husband, Allen, called to tell me that finally a baby might be available for us to adopt.

We wasted no time in contacting the attorney handling the case. We quickly discovered the deadline was *now*. The birth mother would collect the applications that afternoon. With the clock ticking, I answered the questions about why we would make good parents.

Several weeks went by, with no word.

One rainy afternoon, I saw Cindy, who worked with the attorney, at the post office. I asked, "Have you heard anything?"

With downcast eyes, she answered, "I'm sorry. The birth mother picked up the applications, but she has disappeared."

Disappointed, I relayed the news to Allen.

Over the months ahead, I pondered on what might have been and wondered about the birth mother.

In December, I received an unexpected phone call from Cindy. She exclaimed, "The girl is back in town, and she selected you and Allen!"

Our lives had never been more chaotic. We both had full-time careers, and Allen had added the extra duties of becoming mayor of our town. Still we were thrilled about the "possibility," even though we were warned over and over not to get our hopes up. But how could we not?

So the countdown began.

At once I wanted to order nursery wallpaper, until Allen pleaded, "Please, Debbie, no decorating and no baby showers. You'll be too disappointed if it doesn't work out." Instead we took care of the financial and medical arrangements. A social worker inspected our home—and us. There were mandatory physicals, including checkups for venereal diseases.

This last experience led me to ask our attorney to obtain a family health history from the birth mother. The request resulted in a series of notes that bounced back and forth on index cards between the mother and me. Eventually, our correspondence shifted away from discussions of health. She asked, "What do you consider a *happy* home? A *good* education? *Appropriate* discipline?"

Little by little, I began to think like a mother. Together we were preparing for the birth of the baby—hers and mine.

And oddly enough, this stranger turned into a friend.

Though neither of us wanted to meet, our notes revealed that we shared similar interests, such as the theater, walking on the beach, and reading. Even our printing looked identical. I also discovered that she was articulate, humorous, mature, and selfless in her desire to provide a loving family for her baby.

One cold February day, I received a jubilant call from Cindy. She said, "Congratulations! You have a baby girl!"

"Is she OK? How is the mother?" I was ecstatic.

"They are both fine—just fine," Cindy said, laughing.

Tears streaming down my face, I called Allen. I could barely get the words out. "We have a baby girl!"

Within hours, everyone in our small town knew about the birth of our baby. Friends loaned us a car seat and a cradle. Onlookers watched as we raced from store to store, piling our buggy high with pink diapers, tiny smocked dresses, sleepers, and soft pastel blankets.

Meanwhile, the birth mother held the baby, making sure she was healthy. She was adamant that no one adopt her but us.

In less than twenty-four hours, bouquets of flowers arrived by the dozen and pink balloons floated above our mailbox. Best of all, our baby daughter came home with us.

Meredith gripped her daddy's finger as I slipped off her socks to count her ten tiny toes. "This little piggy went to market," I cooed, as Allen laughed. "And her nose looks like yours," I said. In fact, Meredith did look like him!

As I dug into the hospital's gift bag, I saw the final letter from my friend, tucked beneath the baby wipes and the lotion. I wasn't able to open it just yet.

Falling in love with Meredith came naturally, but I did not expect to feel love for a stranger when Allen and I decided to adopt; and I did—I came to love the birth mother. Thankfully, Meredith would always be our bond.

So with tears flowing, I read her love-filled note, which ended, "I gave her life, now you give her love." My note back would have said, "We always will!"

DEBRA AYERS BROWN

SURROGATE DREAMER

I was annoyed when the phone rang, as I was trying to get dinner going and finish a research paper due the following day. It was the long-awaited finals week of my graduate program. I considered letting the call go to the message machine but changed my mind. It was my best friend, Janice, telling me that Stephen, her husband, was dead; he had died a few hours earlier in her arms of heart failure while they were out dancing.

The night before, I had invited Janice and Stephen for dinner. Since weekends were my main study times, it was rare for me to plan even a small dinner party—especially the week before finals—but I felt a strong need to see them. I reasoned that it was just an informal get-together with longtime friends. Besides, my husband and I were eager to hear about their recent trip to the Caribbean—a celebratory cruise that marked their tenth wedding anniversary. They were deeply in love, like teenagers, really, and they cherished each other.

Instinctively, I had prepared Stephen's favorite meal: grilled fillets, salad, mashed potatoes, and key lime pie. Lingering unusually late, we ventured into long and deep conversation after dinner. Upon reflection, there was a sense of completion and deeper bonding that evening with these two special people; we also made plans to all go to the Caribbean on a mutual vacation the following spring. Stephen was a large bear of a man and gave the warmest of hugs. I wish I'd known when they left, just past midnight, that the good-bye hugs were to be our last from him.

Instead of taking finals, I devoted the next few days to assisting Janice with the details that surround an unexpected death. Stephen was only forty-four. Amid shock and emotional waves of coping, there were multitudes of decisions and logistics of living to consider. The intensity of the experience was overwhelming, but the spiritual beliefs we shared were a luminous glow in the darkness of our grief. Stephen was beloved by all who knew him, and the outpouring of love, caring, and help to Janice allowed me to shift my attention back to school.

Janice hoped to reach Stephen through her dreams—to connect with him as a vital and vibrant form—but she couldn't. Knowing that emotions can block dreams, I reassured her that they would return when she was stronger.

Three days after the funeral, Stephen came to me in a vivid dream, wearing the tuxedo—complete with cummerbund—he had taken on the cruise with Janice. I saw him perfectly; radiant, smiling, and robust. I noticed his shoes especially—highly polished and very formal. I thought this odd, as Stephen had been a very casual person, who rarely wore a tie, much less a suit.

Janice was quiet when I told her about the dream. Unknown to me, she had decided to have Stephen cremated the day before and had dressed him in the clothes he was wearing in my dream. The shoes were one of several pairs he had just purchased. It was as if this detail underlined the authenticity of the dream experience. It was the first of many.

In another dream, Stephen, walking on the beach, delivered a specific message for Janice to listen to John Denver's "Annie's Song." He handed over the cassette.

I told Janice about the dream the next morning. We shed sweet tears as we listened to the lyrics of the song together. "Let me drown in your laughter, let me die in your arms..." I'm convinced Janice was able to heal more easily knowing Stephen was watching over her in a personal way.

Until Janice was able to dream of him on her own, I became the "surrogate dreamer." Our close friendship ties and love for each other provided fertile links for dream communication that were not available to Janice in her swollen emotional state. As her grief lessened, her dreams and images of Stephen returned. Mine began to diminish, and they came to a remarkable culmination a few years later during my trip with my husband to the

Caribbean in the spring. We toasted him—"Bon voyage"—as we traveled the itinerary that we had planned together the night before he died.

Marlene L. King

SPECIAL DELIVERY

I had been seeing Josh for over a year and a half. He was my first love, tall and handsome, with a boyish smile. He had an uncanny way of making everyone around him laugh, especially me. I adored him.

Josh was a master of surprises. He had a unique and wonderful way of expressing his feelings. I would often find roses at my door or notes on my car windshield. On one occasion, he dropped by my apartment in a new four-door brown sedan. As we walked toward the car, he explained to me that its best feature was a large trunk. How could he be so excited about a trunk, when the car had so many other interesting gadgets? As he lifted the back hatch, I realized why the trunk was so special. In it lay a dozen red roses for me.

Needless to say, when Josh said he was planning a surprise for my twenty-fourth birthday, my imagination ran wild. At this point, we were carrying on a long-distance relationship, he in Connecticut and I in Wisconsin.

Three days before my birthday, Josh called to find out where I was going to be on the eve of my birthday.

"On the eve of my birthday?" I asked. "What's so important about the eve of my birthday?"

He explained to me that his present would arrive at approximately 12:01 A.M. on October 14, my birthday. He wanted his present to be the first one I received that day.

I told him he would never find a service that delivered packages twenty-four hours a day.

"On the contrary," he said. "I deal with many companies that deliver twenty-four hours a day, seven days a week." He told me to expect a package from Russell's Expedite Service on October 14 at 12:01 A.M.

I think I counted the hours, maybe the minutes, to the eve of my birthday. What could possibly top the airplane ticket and homemade videos of Boston's beautiful fall foliage from last year's birthday?

Josh checked in with me the morning of the thirteenth. I told him I would call him as soon as the package was dropped off.

I worked late that evening and arrived home at nine. My roommate and I decided to relax and watch television until the package arrived. Finally, though, tired after a long day, we both decided to head to bed. It was about eleven-thirty.

"I can't imagine that he found a place that would deliver twenty-four hours a day," I told her, not for the first time. "It'll be here tomorrow morning."

Just as we were about to turn off the lights, the door buzzer rang. My heart jumped. We ran to the front of our building, pajamas and all, and flung the door open.

"Are you Lisa?" asked the delivery woman who stood before us. "Yes," I said.

She said, "I have a package for you."

And with those words, from around the corner came my "special delivery" from Russell's Expedite Service. It was Josh! Josh, the master of surprise and champion of making a woman feel special. He was truly my first present of the day!

Josh and I both have new loves in our lives now, but his memory lingers on. Because of Josh and his great efforts to please me, I now pay attention to the surprises I can create for the special people I love. Josh was a teacher to me. He taught me at an early age that when it comes to matters of the heart, *little things are big things.*

LISA JUSCIK

RITUALS THAT TOUCH THE HEART

Recently, I spoke at a conference with Mary LoVerde. She focuses on how family rituals touch our lives. Knowing that we are all teachers to one another, we asked the women in the audience to share rituals they have in their families.

To set the tone, I described a family ritual that has had a lasting impact on my life from the time I was a young girl. My father began writing poems to us with each Christmas present he gave. The whole family writes poems now, and each year our Christmas experience lasts all morning as the extended family—our sons, their wives, cousins, aunts and uncles—take turns reading a poem they've been given as a gift.

As our kids grew up, they started with simple poems like "Roses are red, violets are blue . . ." Often the poems give hints of what's inside the wrapping. It's been fascinating to watch the young poets develop. Last year our twenty-three-year-old son, Rick, got a round of applause for this one: "Stuck with yourself in stormy bad weather, / outside your house with cotton, not leather. / Thinking of old times as the rain wets your head, / you remember last Christmas—all the loot, all the bread. / One gift stands out from Xmas '96, / it's that nice gift from me, old Ricky-Pix. . . ." And on it went. . . .

Over the years, the poems collected have become a lifetime treasury. While the actual gift may well be forgotten as time has passed, the poems are not. These gems are carefully stored in a small chest. If a fire were to ever break out in our home, that chest, with its special contents, would be one of the first things I would attempt to save.

Ten years ago, my husband placed an unopened pouch of Sweet Dreams brand tea in my jacket pocket. It was a way for him to say, "I'm thinking of you" whether he's home or traveling. Without a word, we continue to take turns exchanging that now rumpled tea bag in each other's clothes hanging in our closet. When I find it in one of my jacket pockets, I wait awhile, then return it to one of his. I never know when that "sweet" message will make me smile again!

Recently I gave my daughter-in-law a decorative wheelbarrow to put on her front porch. I have one too. We are creating a tradition of getting together to fill our wheelbarrows with seasonal delights, like pumpkins near Halloween and holly at Christmastime.

After I told my stories, the women began describing to us a number of their cherished rituals. One gives each of her children a back rub each night when she tucks them into bed. Another woman takes a bite out of the sandwich she packs in her husband's daily lunch! Even when they're not together during the day, they are connected.

Another woman moved me deeply when she stood up and shared with all of us how difficult it had been for her to be a long distance away from her young granddaughter. She wanted to feel close to her but didn't know how. This grandmother waited until the perfect solution revealed itself. She called her granddaughter with an idea that has since become a ritual between the two of them. "I love you so much," she told the young child, "and I have a way that we can feel close to each other all the time! Each night at bedtime, look out your window up at the sky and find the moon. Whenever you see the moon, think of me. And when I go to bed at night, I'll look out my window, find the moon, and think of you."

I've learned to pay attention to the meaningful ways we can get close to the people we love through rituals. From simple deeds to grand gestures, the richness of our lives is proportionate to the gifts we give from our hearts.

KAY ALLENBAUGH

LESSON FOR A LIFETIME

"*If* they steal it, they steal it," Tim, my trusting husband, said as he went off to shower and get ready for dinner.

Our moving van was locked tight under a security light in the motel parking lot. I attributed my anxiety to exhaustion after hours of driving, punctuated with children's questions and my tears. We were leaving Cincinnati, where we'd had lots of friends and a church that meant much to our family. Bittersweet emotions accompanied us as Tim drove the van and we followed in the car.

When we stopped in Corbin, Kentucky, for gas, Tim and the girls decided we should celebrate our anniversary, an occasion we had barely noticed. We had fourteen years of marriage to celebrate, plus we were moving home to Georgia, to our family and an exciting ministry on the campus of the university.

The next morning Tim dressed early and went to check on the truck. As I was braiding J. J.'s hair, he burst back in the room, saying he couldn't find the van.

"What do you mean, you can't find it?" I said. "How can you lose a twenty-four-foot moving van?" The words tumbled out of my mouth, and I wanted to recall them immediately as I saw color drain from his face. Missy began to cry. She knew from his tone that Daddy wasn't teasing. The seriousness of the situation began to sink in.

The hours followed in a blur. The police came and asked a lot of questions. We telephoned the van company, our family, and various insurance companies. We returned to our room after a valiant effort to eat breakfast and make a list of the moving truck's contents. All the while, a giant cold fist grew larger and larger in the pit of my stomach. Reality was settling in. When my brain began functioning, the panic started. What would we do? How could we survive? We had no savings—so how could we replace anything?

Tim suggested that we pray. I didn't feel like praying, and I suspect he really didn't, either. Nevertheless, we joined hands and prayed humbly and simply. Amid sniffles and sobs, we asked for our things to be returned. We praised God that no one was injured and that we had each other—our real treasure. Only the passing traffic broke the morning silence as we waited.

That afternoon, we received a call from the police: they had recovered our truck on a back road. Our hopes soared! When we arrived at the abandoned van, we found only Tim's desk and a few cartons of books. Only later did we realize that Tim had just what he needed to get started in his new ministry. More resources would follow.

I couldn't contain my tears as I picked up love letters strewn over the truck bed. This violation of my privacy was more than I could bear. I searched through the boxes of books and papers for our daughters' baby books and my wedding album, but they weren't there. Who would do something like this? Who would want to take things that had no real value other than sentiment?

It's been fifteen years, and each time I recount this story, I marvel at the response of friends, acquaintances, family, and strangers. In an outpouring of love, we received more than $16,000 in cash, plus clothes, household goods, pantry items, toys, bicycles, appliances, and tons of cards and letters.

The theft of our moving van is a benchmark for us. We speak of events as "before the theft" or "after the theft." It is and will always be a significant event in our family's history, but it isn't a negative one. In many ways, it was a "blessed theft," for in the removal of the weight of worldly possessions, we learned the lesson of a lifetime—forgiveness.

SHEILA S. HUDSON

X
A DEEPER REFLECTION

"Some days there won't be a song in your heart.
Sing anyway."

—Emory Austin

FOUR WEDDINGS
AND A MIRACLE

*C*hildren do not learn the alphabet in one lesson. It takes time and repetition. So why should we have expected my husband's young children to grasp the meaning of their daddy's marriage to a woman other than their mother with just one ceremony?

Justine and Tyler were seven and five when Doug and I became engaged. After a year of dating, I felt blessed that they welcomed me into their little worlds so openly and lovingly. And yet behind every smile lived a shadow of apprehension. While Justine asked me why storybook stepmothers were always evil and Tyler asked me why his dad and I couldn't just be friends, Doug and I were asking ourselves and each other how to create a wedding ceremony that would help build a new family group. A couple of starry-eyed "I dos" with Pachelbel's Canon playing in the background wasn't enough. That's when we decided to have a series of ceremonies, one at each season of our first year together.

Our first wedding ceremony took place in our living room, in front of a few friends and a raging fire, on the winter solstice of 1994. After the exchange of rings, the minister invited Justine and Tyler to join us at the hearth. It was an opportunity for me to express my love and declare my commitment to them as their stepmother. "Always remember," I said, "you have a mom to mother you and a dad to father you. And now, as your stepmother, my job is to angel you." As a token of my love, I presented them with little glass angels. They went to bed that night, saturated with cake and candy, each clutching a little angel. Before drifting off to sleep,

Justine smiled and whispered to a family friend, "Just think, when I wake up tomorrow morning, Kate will be my stepmom."

So began my life as a stepmother. No one knows except another stepparent how double-edged that (s)word is. The books say to just be a friend. Yet as the first months of stepfamily life unfolded, I found myself taking on more and more parental duties. On the surface, I enjoyed a good relationship with Doug and his kids. But underneath my polished and ever-so-well-read veneer, I began to seethe with the first waves of resentment. I did everything Doug and his ex-wife did, sometimes more, but I never got the rewards. Every time I'd hear Justine declare to her dad, in a little singsongy voice, "I love you, Dad-dee," feelings of irritation would well up until I was dangerously close to shouting, Hey, what about me? I sadly learned at a stepmoms support group meeting that I should get used to those feelings. Words like "I love you" are reserved for the real mom and the real dad. "Nothing short of a miracle will make a child say that to a stepmom, no matter how well liked she is," I was told.

Energized by the first signs of spring, I approached our second wedding ceremony with a renewed sense of confidence and joy. Doug and I repeated our vows to each other in front of a group of two hundred family members and friends. I repeated my vows to Justine and Tyler, honoring their mom and dad, and reminding them about my commitment to angel them. This time I presented them with animal totems—a little wooden fox for Justine and a tiny furry mouse for Tyler. They were so excited they practically snatched the little critters out of my hand.

Summer rolled around and so did ceremony number three, this one with my family in Iowa. For a third time, I repeated my vows to Doug and his children. I presented Justine and Tyler with small dreamcatchers, Native American art pieces, explaining that as I angeled them, I'd help them catch their dreams. They proudly hung them above their beds in the tiny motel room, then began to reminisce about the series of ceremonies and symbols I had given them.

Overwhelmed by the weariness of traveling with kids and sharing my purse, pockets, and pup tent of a motel room with them, I felt myself growing a little distant. I was spending an enormous amount of energy trying to resist the temptation to wallow in self-pity.

We took the kids for a twilight walk near a cornfield for their first glimpse of fireflies, or lightning bugs, as we used to call them. It was a Disney moment, the field aglitter with little beings of light performing an ancient aerial ballet. If you listened closely, you could hear the soft strains of a cricket sonata. The air was heavy with humidity and the aroma of summer grasses. Suddenly, without warning, Justine came up and took my hand. We walked along the dusty country road, silently sharing the splendor of this real-life field of dreams. And then she said it—quietly and sweetly, in that singsongy voice reserved for her dad: "I love you, Kate." A million fireflies flew out of my heart as I responded, "I love you too, Justine." She was quiet for a moment and visibly nervous. Finally, she confessed, "I've always wanted to say that to you, but I was afraid if I loved you it meant I wouldn't love my mom." I asked her if she understood the difference now. She said yes, and that she understood the similarities as well.

That fall, the fourth and final ceremony took place, back in our living room, with the same people from the first wedding. We celebrated the autumn equinox by honoring the harvest and restating our personal vows. This time I gave the kids bigger animals, in honor of the bigger love we now shared—a unicorn for Justine and a big mouse for Tyler.

Just like learning the alphabet, I believe it took the time and repetition of our four wedding ceremonies for the kids to become familiar with our new family group. And not just the kids, but Doug and me as well. Now when the hard times hit, instead of letting my feelings run from A to Z, I can reflect on the rhythms of the seasons and remember that special summer night in Iowa. There will be no more wedding ceremonies, but the summer fireflies that live in my heart all year round are already preparing for more miracles.

KATE MCKERN VERIGIN

DOES THE BREAST HAVE A SOUL?

It had been three weeks since I heard the dreaded news: I had extensive breast cancer. The doctors estimated I'd had it for at least two years. The tumor was large, and based on my consultation with many doctors, my options were limited. My breast would have to be removed. It didn't take long for me to think of my children and husband and decide to go ahead with surgery. But the thought of losing a part of my body would not penetrate into my psyche. For days before the surgery, I would stand in front of the mirror, looking at both my breasts, trying to picture what it would be like to have only one. I would cover one up and turn this way and that, as if I were trying on a new dress.

This cancer did not come at a convenient time—not that anything of this nature ever does. My international sales company was in the process of launching a major new product in the Pacific Rim. We would be meeting with fifteen distributors in Thailand in only five days. As I sat at my desk, knee deep in brochures, manuals, and travel arrangements, it was amazing how fast the Bangkok meeting, the urgent crises in the office, the constant demands of the outside world, all disappeared. All that mattered now was my survival and spending time with my family. I dropped everything, suddenly saying no to those tasks and people I simply did not want to spend time on. For the first time in my career, I did not tell my family I had too much work to do, that I couldn't cook dinner for them or take my children to a movie or go out for dinner with my husband. For the first time, I said, "Work will wait, my family won't."

On the morning before surgery, I went out to breakfast with one of my good friends. I sat there watching him eat his bacon and eggs, and I said again and again, "I don't want to do this. I want to be someplace else. I don't want to lose my breast." As I cried, he stroked my head like a parent comforting a small child. "It's only skin," he said. "It's not important." But the tears continued, not out of fear of the surgery but from fear of losing a part of myself. "How do you know I'll be the same person when this is over? What if I lose part of who I am?"

My friend comforted me until it was time to go to the hospital. My parents had flown across the country to be with me, and my husband was going to come from work to join us. We all gathered in my room, but in the hour before the surgery, I was very restless. I asked everyone to leave. My mind was not settled. The nurses tried to give me a tranquilizer, but I refused. "No, I have to sort this out in my mind."

Then it occurred to me: "Does the breast have a soul? Am I killing off something that is as much a living thing as I am?" I knew what I must do. I must say thank you and goodbye to my breast.

I searched the hospital room, found an old envelope, and asked the nurse for a pencil. Again she tried to get a tranquilizer down me, but I knew that it would cloud my brain. I was determined to write down what was going through my mind. Almost everyone had told me, "It's only skin—it's not necessary." But that's not what I felt. I felt it was part of me and I was part of it. I asked myself, "Where are my feelings? Are they only in my heart?"

I kept thinking: How do these people know my soul is not in my breast? Before they took it away, I wanted to move the part of who I was that was in there somewhere else.

I wanted to thank my breast for what it had given me. It had helped me to know that I was passing from girlhood to womanhood. It had nursed my babies and fed them well. It had given me shape. It had pleased my husband and it had pleased me. Could I be whole without it? Or was I still angry at it for betraying me? It was as if my breast had plotted against me: me, who had taken care of it all these years . . . me, who had taken such pride in it. How could my breast turn on me like this? Many years ago, when I was out of college and moving into the world on my own, I told my parents they must let go of me. It was time. Was I ready to say good-bye to my breast in the same way? Could I say, "It's time"?

Now I began visualizing the part of me that resided in my breast moving into my arms, my legs, my stomach, and my heart. Just as I finished, I heard the gurney at the door. They had come to separate me from my breast. I looked at the nurse peacefully and said, "It's OK, it's time. I've mourned my breast. I've said thank you. I've moved the part of my soul that's in my breast to other places in my body. They can take it away. After all, it's only skin."

Lynne Massie

> "A successful marriage requires falling in love many times, always with the same person."
> —Mignon McLughlin

ALL THAT GLITTERS

Oh, yeah, I remember him. Mom didn't approve, but I did—Sam Elliott in a tux, silver mane of hair slicked back into a ponytail, mustachioed and smelling of Brut. He was the embodiment of cool. I'm not sure if he was cooler in his Christmas tux or strung long-legged over the seat of his Harley shovelhead. I slipped in behind him and dreamed *bad-boy* dreams, my arms wrapped around his waist like a brand-new belt. He was everything my mother never wanted for me.

Now, Mom loved the CEO I dated. In Armani and toting a six-figure income strapped to his side like a modern-day cowboy, he had a ponytail too, but clipped and très chic, just enough to keep him young. A real boardroom Brad Pitt. I walked the manufacturing line with him once, and when I saw how far away he stood when he talked to the welders and grinders and women in the finishing room, I found myself slipping out. Again.

Find a nice man! Settle down! My girlfriends and I ran from the persistent pleas of our mothers, and spending time in local singles bars and restaurants, trying to look nonchalant, we swept eager eyes over clenched crowds of suited, sweet-smelling men. Hey, is that him? Tossing hands through carefully casual hair and checking our butts with a back glance in the mirror, we pretended it didn't matter. It was 1992, and a woman didn't need a man to feel complete. So why'd we keep on looking?

Because somewhere the threads of the fairy tale still sweep off the spindle, and we keep hoping there's more out there for us than Rumpelstiltskins and dwarfs. Where did that prince get to anyway?

So the day I lifted my head up from a bucket of parts in my own factory job and fell in love from across the room, it was with more than just a little surprise. I mean, for a girl raised on magnolias, white gloves, Southern sun, and Scarlett tales, who'd have thought love would come in the form of a broad-shouldered Vermonter with the conversational skills of Gary Cooper. It took a while to realize that "yep" meant "I love you too."

But sweeter than maple sap, he is as solid as Vermont granite, solemnly funny, and heartbreakingly New England practical. He can fix anything with a motor, builds killer science projects for kids he loves unswervingly, and possesses a reverence for nature as timeless as the Green Mountains that bore him. Most at home in silence, he maneuvers through a loud Southern family with quiet grace, smiling where others would guffaw, and speaking only when he has something to say.

Sometimes I trace the smattering of freckles across his chest, connecting the dots until they form the Big Dipper, and in the secure blanket of his stillness, the miracle of love burns my throat with tears. Intricate in its simplicity. No flash. Just pure sweet honest substance.

He could have been a gas station attendant, a tax accountant, a landscaper. But what if I'd kept looking for Sam Elliott? I might have looked right past my man. I watch him while he's sleeping, the tired deep sleep of a man who works hard to care for his family. And sometimes I try to picture what he'd look like on a Harley. But then again, why mess with perfection?

MARY CARROLL-HACKETT

A NEW DEAL

Three years ago, I wrote the following journal entry: *There is only silence. Silence, once my most desirable ally, is now the thing I dread most. I have isolated myself into paralysis. I sort wash, collect groceries, answer phone calls, love the children and my husband, but something is missing.*

I have tried counseling, God, meditation, and even with all this I am still depressed. Turning myself into a highway fatality is not the answer, but the temptation is strong. I've exhausted all options to cure my depression except for one: drugs. Today is the day I am going to ask for professional help, for a reference to a psychiatrist.

A month later, the psychiatrist sat me in a cloth-covered peach chair with a good five feet of pond-green carpet between us. She sat, legs crossed at the knee, in an upright mahogany desk chair, with a clipboard in her lap, and she spent eighty minutes asking me questions and jotting copious notes.

I would have walked out if she had not been my last resort. Throughout the "evaluation," I searched for some sign that she had a life as well. There were no pictures of children, no wall-mounted plaques of achievement, only her doctorate diploma, its printing too small for me to read from where I sat. The plants in the room were silk, the vertical blinds were drawn against the afternoon sun. It was a room nothing could die in, because there wasn't enough life to make a decent death.

At the end of the interview, she took my $175, wrote me a receipt, and gave me the good news: I was clinically depressed, and "in view of the diagnosis, help is available." She unlocked an upright cream file cabinet and handed me a psychic Band-Aid of marsh-green-and-cream capsules suspended in shrink-wrapped cellophane, together with a leaflet explaining side effects and benefits. I stuffed it all in the bottom of my purse.

The next day I combed the library for articles and books on

Prozac. The only book I found was *Listening to Prozac*. *Time* and *Newsweek* articles were abundant. The only article with any meat to it was a thirteen-pager in *Psychology Today*, titled "The Transformation of Personality."

I copied the article and wondered whether I wanted my personality altered. I knew I didn't want to be depressed anymore: my husband was reading up on life insurance policies, and my kids prefaced every conversation with, "I don't want you to cry, but . . ." Yet fractured as it was, it was my personality. Did I want to trade it in on someone nobody knew, even though what little energy I had went into dragging one foot in front of the other? I imagined the scene: "Let's make a deal," the psychiatrist says. "I'll trade you your depression for what's behind door number two." The audience screams conflicting advice, and in the end I have to make up my own mind. "The door," I say. And with that the curtain is whisked back to reveal Vanna White draped against a pedestal of Prozac. "These pills won't change your personality," the grinning psychiatrist says. "They'll change your life."

So I went to counseling, meditated, prayed, and took Prozac. I still felt some resistance: I'm used to doing for myself. Drugs were for people who were too weak to do it on their own. From teenhood, I'd known depression's rhythms and cycles. I was always on guard for that initial downslide, which still came as a surprise. A month into taking Prozac, I wasn't sure, but I thought I felt better.

Six months into life with Prozac, I searched less often for the signs of downslide, almost trusting myself to make long-term plans. Plans for a job, for a sailing vacation in the Caribbean, for old age—which I might even see.

A year down the road, I was hired for a job as a teacher's assistant in my kids' primary school. I worked half-time, cooked, played, ate, wrote, and loved. It was as if someone had taken the plastic wrap off my serving bowl and for the first time in my life I had a clear shot at the food.

Two years later, I was working full time, with enjoyable people, health benefits, and good pay. But a nattering at the back of my mind turned into a din as weeks flew by. I wanted to quit my job and write. I knew it was possible. Possible because the bottom no longer fell out from under me. Possible because at a time when I was at my lowest, I asked for help. Taking Prozac or any drug to help clear away depression's fog is as essential for some people as setting a broken arm. It has not been a substitute for asking myself the hard questions and acting on the answers; it has not transformed my personality; but it has placed solid ground where there once was none.

It took me a week to confide in my family my dream to write. They supported me fully. I quit my job the next day. I was ready to make a new deal. Ready to step out of silence and write my way home.

BURKY ACHILLES

> "Time will outweigh the moment."
> —Demi Moore

ENTRANCES AND EXITS

When I became pregnant with Nicole, friends kept telling me the pain of childbirth would be easily forgotten in the joy and love of parenting. They were right. Our lives were forever changed for the better the day Nicole entered the world. The moments surrounding her birth are forever etched clearly in my mind, minus the pain.

Nearly eighteen years later, when she chose to end her own life suddenly on a dreary day in February, other grieving parents gathered my husband, Scott, and me within their embrace. They looked into our eyes and said the pain would get better with time, even though our lives would now forever be divided into "before" and "after." Again we found the words of friends to be correct, though the pain of parting was so much more intense and enduring than any labor contraction.

Having worked in public schools as a speech/language clinician for sixteen years, I suddenly found myself with a communication disorder of epic proportions—a development that I could attribute only to my grief and ever-present anxiety. I now panicked at my thickened tongue, my scattered thought processing, and my slurred speech. Even my nonwaking moments were haunted. I had always enjoyed frequent and vivid dreams. I was now afraid to go to sleep, in fear of what I might dream.

Nicole's presence in our lives had brought such joy that we'd tried to have other children, but we were not successful. After her death, approaching the middle years of our lives, we found ourselves shocked, numb, devastated, and dreadfully alone.

We lacked energy to do even the most normal of tasks, and our ability to concentrate vanished, except when it came to books. We read voraciously, eager to learn all we could about suicide in our search to answer "why?" Scott and I clung together, defying the grim statistics of marriage splits following the death of a child. We also joined suicide survivor support groups, driving great distances to attend meetings. From these I slowly regained the ability to verbalize thoughts, and we began to unravel small threads of the mysterious tapestry surrounding our daughter's death. We asked the usual "what if"s and pieced facts together, never really finding an answer. Nicole had given precious few clues to us or any of her friends of any existing depression. Up until the time of her death, she had been happy, loving, caring, kind, and active in school and church. Maybe if she *had* been a bit more of a rebel . . . but "what if"s are useless. We have come to accept that perhaps the suicidal mind needs medication just as the diabetic needs insulin.

We were fortunate to be surrounded by family, friends, colleagues, and a community that let us share our grief openly. Their hugs restored our energy, their gifts of food restored our appetites, and their calls broke deafening silences.

And when my dreams resumed, I found them to be comforting also. In my very first dream, Nicole's favorite color—sea green—enveloped me. Not too long afterward, she was giving me a hug. Once, she strolled with me along an ethereal garden path lined with fresh flowers.

As our energy levels returned, Scott and I found that traveling over major holidays and significant dates helped us survive better. We discovered we could even laugh again, but we agreed that life was now like a tree without tinsel.

Grief is different for everyone. Finding reasons to go on can be difficult but is necessary. If you are fortunate enough, a point may be reached in the grieving and healing process when you no longer would trade the future to change the past. This began for us three Februarys following Nicole's death, when we adopted two remarkable babies—our son, Tony, and our daughter, Gina. The four of us have begun anew.

We don't have time to worry that we are old enough to be their grandparents, and a day never passes that we aren't thankful for the entrance of all three children into our lives.

Will these beloved babies ever keep us from missing Nicole? No, never. But we look back at our time of deepest pain, and that makes this new delight so much more appreciated. To enter the highest joys, we have found you sometimes have to walk through and exit the deepest of sorrows.

LINDA G. ENGEL

FOR BETTY

"Good things come to those who wait," he had lectured on too many occasions. It was his favorite saying, and even as I backed the car away from the house and the life we had built together, he stood silent in the driveway, just waiting.

It was his nature to wait, as he did throughout the troubled moments of our marriage. He said nothing and did nothing as he waited out the storms. Living with me was like being a passenger on a runaway train, and we traveled different paths at different paces. In my youth and impatience, I had yet to discover myself, and soon it became clearly inevitable that we should part.

In the months of separation before the divorce, I shuttled back and forth, searching for confirmation of what I already knew. I wore out the skies from the state I had moved to and back home again, in search of an answer. We had been through counseling, we had been through it all, yet our differences were basic and beyond repair. We both knew it, but neither of us could make the final move, so our lives lingered unfairly in purgatory for several years, as time drifted slowly away.

On one of my frequent flights back home, I sat next to Betty, a vivacious woman of sixty-five. I soon learned that Betty was traveling first class because the airplane had upgraded her following her son's death. Her only child had been a pilot for the airline, until he called her one day to report a "strange sensation," which turned out to be a brain tumor. Sadly, he died soon after. Not only that, said Betty, but her husband had worked and saved his entire life so that they could travel the world together when he retired. He did retire, but he died unexpectedly just weeks later, and the plans they had made would never be realized.

Betty and I talked for the duration of the flight. "I don't know how there could be a God," she said bitterly. "Everything I ever loved is gone. I have no children, I have no husband, I have nothing at all. If there is any advice I can give you, it's to do it now. Don't wait until it's too late to do the things you want to do in life."

Weeks later, I found myself thinking about Betty and the advice she had given. I also found the strength to move on, away from the relationship that wasn't right and into the next phase of my life. It is years later, and I still think of Betty and thank her for that morning we spent together on the airplane. I know I will live a fuller life because of it, and I know that I'll never delay the things I want to achieve. Good things might come to those who wait, but great things happen to those who refuse to.

TAMMY KLING

UNITED STATES OF MOTHERHOOD

The luminous numbers clicked as the time moved from 1:59 A.M. to 2:00. I shifted the weight on my lap and moved my son from one breast to the other.

Quickly Michael made it clear that he was no longer interested in nursing. I shifted him to my shoulder and patted his warm little back, waiting for that satisfying burp that would signal his stomach's acceptance of my late-night offerings. Beneath me, I felt my legs growing numb and tingly. Even with a cushion, this wooden rocker was painful to sit in for long periods, night after night.

From the light of the streetlamp, I could see shadows in my son's room. The quiet of the evening settled around us, but still Michael wouldn't sleep.

"Colic," said the pediatrician. "We don't know why it happens. He'll grow out of it at about three months. We suspect their digestive system starts to mature by then. You're home free the day he passes gas. Sorry."

Sorry! Sorry? My patience and my body were worn thin. All the baby books had profiled an infant who would spend most of his early first year snoozing.

With my southern hemisphere sporting more stitches than a Quaker's sampler and my hair coming out in chunks, I was a poster child for postpartum distress. My sanity began to unravel as I hallucinated that I was part of an ancient Mayan culture where babies were gourds. The next day, when I dragged myself, baby and car seat in tow, into the pediatrician's office, I had been up forty-eight hours straight. Michael had slept a mere forty-five minutes during that two-day eternity. Thirty of those forty-five minutes had been on the car ride to the clinic. If I could only stay awake long enough, I might be able to drive to Alaska and back in three months.

The drugs to ease Michael's system began, thank goodness, to take effect. His naps fell into a general pattern, though it was far, far shorter than that presented by the experts. But nighttime was party time for Mr. Mike. I read books about letting him scream. I listened to tapes by experts on walking away. I tried gizmos and gadgets that shook me and his bed like a blender on whirl. But I couldn't walk away or relegate him to machinery. He was obviously in distress. The least I could do, I reasoned, was sit with him through the long and painful nights while he squirmed and struggled to fall asleep.

So we rocked. We rocked the circumference of the earth. Then we rocked our way to the moon. Tonight we had been rocking toward Pluto. I brushed the velvety crown of his head. So dear, so soft, like chick down. I curled and uncurled his tiny fingers. I struggled with my anger. I sat there alone with him as my husband slept. Why wasn't the baby sleeping? How long could I go without rest? A wave of shame broke over me. Wasn't I blessed to have him? Wouldn't a million women give anything to be holding a child?

Then, as I glimpsed the moon moving behind a cloud, a thought came to me. A million women. A million mothers. A million babies.

Suddenly I realized that I was not alone. All over the globe, women were holding their babies. Some were lucky enough to sit in rockers. Some crouched on the ground. Some had a roof over their heads, as I did. Many more were exposed to the elements, shielding their babies from the rain, the snow, the sun.

We were all alike. We held our children and prayed. Some would not live to see their children grown. Some children would not live out the year. Some would die of hunger. Some from bullets or sickness.

But for a moment, under the same pale moon, we were all together. Rocking our babies and praying. Loving them and hoping.

From that night on, I viewed my time with Michael differently. The fatigue never left me. The seat never seemed any softer. But as I sat with him, I felt the company of a million, a billion mothers—all holding our babies in our arms.

JOANNA SLAN

XI
SERIOUSLY FUNNY

*"If someone makes me laugh,
I'm [her] slave for life."*

—Bette Midler

A STREAK OF LOVE

One warm spring night on Iraklion Air Station in Crete, I left my dorm with a girlfriend and decided to check out an impromptu party in progress between the two dorms. Boyfriendless at the time, I kind of automatically swept the crowd with my eyes in search of a "potential"—and stopped on Frank.

I'd seen him around the base before, and I'd always thought he was cute. Tall and thin. Curly black hair. Mustache. Kind of Jim Croce–looking. I parked myself next to him and immediately engaged him in conversation.

I found he had a sweet smile and a sexy New York accent. (Terribly exotic for a girl who'd grown up among the cornfields of Indiana.) But it wasn't just his good looks and accent that charmed me. He was a genuinely nice guy, easy to talk to—and best of all, he made me laugh.

I was so engrossed in Frank and his lively conversation that at first I didn't notice the commotion around us. Too late, I looked up in time to see a flash of bare skin disappear around the corner of the building. Everyone laughed hysterically and pointed in that direction. Suddenly I realized what I'd missed.

"My first streakers!" I gasped. Then I turned to Frank accusingly. "And I missed them because of you!"

Frank looked properly contrite. "Sorry. I'll get them to do it again."

I didn't think Frank was serious, but before I could say a word, he scrambled up from the ground and disappeared around the corner of the dorm. A few minutes later, I heard a peal of shrill laughter. I whipped my head around, and there they were—the two streakers, as naked as babes, running like mad demons down the span of lawn between the dorms. The laughter intensified and my eyes widened. A third streaker had joined the other two. He was tall and thin, with curly black hair and a mustache. Kind of Jim Croce–looking.

Oddly enough, Frank missed the whole thing, or so he said. He reappeared at my side a few minutes later as if nothing had happened.

"Thanks," I said dryly. "You didn't have to go to so much trouble to impress me."

He shrugged. "Well, I couldn't let you miss your first streakers."

What could I say? He'd done it for me.

That was the beginning of our relationship. It's been twenty-three years now, and we have two wonderful grown children. Frank doesn't streak anymore. He feels it no longer fits into his lifestyle—him being a respected computer programmer and all. Oh, he still gets naked—just not for the general public.

Everyone who knows the story of our first meeting thinks I saw something I liked that night when Frank streaked past me in the buff. I did.

His personality.

CAROLE BELLACERA

VENUS RISING

When I was seventeen, I spent a few weeks of summer vacation visiting a cousin who lived in the country. It was a far cry from the big city, and every little thing in nature excited me. A barn filled with horses, trails meandering through a dense wooded area, deer, fancy birds, and fish jumping in a nearby lake all created an enchanting environment.

My cousin Jeannie was a tomboy, yet we got along well. She could do all the things the boys on the next farm could do—she shot rabbits, hunted for pheasants, chased wild turkeys, and helped out with farm chores.

Jeannie also played tricks on the boys next door, like the time they went horseback riding. While the guys were in the lake, she rode off with their horses, and they didn't get back to the farmhouse till dinner was over.

One steamy summer morning, I went to the lake by myself. Since no one was around, I took off my clothes and jumped in. I floated on my back just looking up at the clouds through overhanging trees, appreciating wildflowers along the bank. My gosh, it was so beautiful. The birds never sounded more musical, and for a little while I thought this surely was Heaven. I was happy and totally carefree. It felt as though I were swimming in warm velvet.

Suddenly I heard the crackle of branches on the ground and the movement of grass. I ducked down in the water up to my chin and peered into the nearby trees. Out of the green, I recognized Dusty, one of the boys from the neighboring farm. Coming toward the lake, he began to laugh when he saw my look of total surprise. He plopped down on the ground and made himself comfortable My eyes shot to the spot where my clothes were. I said *were!* They were, of course, gone!

"What have you done with my clothes?" I hollered. Dusty just sat there and said, "They ain't far. All you has to do is c'mon out and fetch 'em."

"If you don't give me my clothes, I'll tell my uncle when I get back, and then you'll be in real trouble!"

"Oh, yeah. I reckon so—that is, when you *git* back. See, unless you c'mon out, they ain't no way you'a gon' git back."

This went on for several minutes, and I realized my frustration won out. I couldn't help but cry. Now I hated the lake. Nothing seemed beautiful anymore. Frantically, I looked around for something to hold up in front of me so I could get onto dry ground. But what? A broken bough of branches perhaps . . . something . . . *anything!* I felt a slow surge of panic creep into my throat. I had no idea just how far this charade would go, as Dusty laughed even louder. Should I stay in the water that now felt cold and slimy, or should I make a run for it?

I waded to a nearby marshy area in the lake, hoping to find something. My foot struck a hard yet round object. I reached down to pick it up. It was a rusty enamel pan—just large enough to cover up the lower part of my body. Thank heaven! The pan appeared to be caked with rust and mud, but so what? I put it in front of me and crossing one arm over my chest, I tossed back my head and proceeded to walk out of the water to gather my clothes. I'll show *him,* I thought.

As I walked toward the shore, I snapped, "I'll bet you thought I couldn't get out of this lake!"

Dusty squinted his eyes and stared at me. Slowly he drawled, "Yeaaah, and I'll betcha you thought that pan had a bottom in it!"

CARMEN D'AMICO

WHEN WILL I BE THIN?

While standing in the locker room
    After training at the gym,
My girlfriend turned and said to me,
    "Oh, when will I be thin?"

I said to her, "You're gorgeous!
    There's more to life than looks—
A woman with a soul on fire
    Is one who really cooks!"

When you're feeling kinda funky
    And your chin's a little low,
Just use this little motto—
    Here's the way it goes:

Though our perky breasts may fall
    And our youthful skin may wrinkle,
What we have within our souls
    Is an everlasting twinkle!

So never doubt you're beautiful,
    Don't ever question that.
'Cause a soulful woman's gorgeous,
    Though her thighs are fat.

So don't give up the truffles
    If they're your heart's delight,
Just jog an extra mile
    While you twinkle in God's light.

MAUREEN GORSUCH

THE GREAT ZUCCHINI CAPER

He'd been on vacation only three days, and already the man was driving me crazy. My husband, Stan, usually oblivious to an overflowing trash can or squeaky doors, became an overzealous combination of Mr. Fix-It and Mr. Clean. He insisted on tidying every nook and cranny. He even took out the garbage with the rotten zucchini in it and placed a new paper bag in the trash can.

Used to having my mornings to myself, I especially needed some quiet time this particular day so I could review my program for a new client I hoped to impress. My employer was collaborating with a large franchise, and the chance for additional business looked promising. I'd spread the papers and documents entrusted to me across my coffee table, when my husband hit me with a barrage of suggestions.

"Let's get this place cleaned up, then take the boys for a ride in the country. We'll fish, have a picnic, pick some wild berries. . . . Come on, let's get cracking."

I finally conceded. Maybe togetherness and relaxation would do us all good. I felt keyed up and needed a little distraction.

As we headed out the door, I noticed that the coffee table was empty. "Stan," I began cautiously, "where are the papers that were on this table?"

"I don't know." His impatience sounded loud and clear. "I couldn't stand the clutter, so I cleared it off."

"But what did you do with my papers?" I persisted, my voice rising as my heart began to quicken.

"If they were on the table, then they probably got pitched in the trash along with the Sunday paper."

It was trash day, but the collectors weren't due for another couple of hours. I walked outside and stopped dead in my tracks. Two empty trash cans leered at me like a pair of hollow eyes. I stared into them, unable to comprehend the obvious. Then it hit me like a train engine crashing into my chest.

My valuable papers had been tossed away carelessly with the Sunday paper and the rotten zucchini and were now being carried off to God knows where. I tried to choke off my scream as I bolted into the house.

My husband's eyes grew wide as I stormed past. "What's the matter?"

"You threw away my outline, my notes, my objectives—everything! Don't you understand? You threw away my papers, and I don't know if they can be replaced. The administrator won't understand. He'll never believe I could be so incompetent." I ran to our bedroom and slammed the door and then, feeling the need for further isolation, locked myself in the bathroom. For several minutes, tears flooded down my cheeks, drenching the toilet paper I clutched tightly in my hand.

I kept asking myself whatever was I going to do. Then it struck me. It was obvious: there was only one thing I could do. Without an explanation to anyone, I raced out the door—no makeup, hair flying in all directions, dressed in my "farm" clothes. I jumped into my small station wagon and peeled out of the driveway.

As I barreled down the street, one thought crowded out all others: I have to find my papers. I got to the first intersection, when an overwhelming realization smacked me between the eyes. I had absolutely no idea where to start looking for the garbage man, what his route was, or even what his truck looked like. He could be anywhere by now.

I gazed toward the heavens, searching for some divine sign, and recognizing none, I took a fifty-fifty chance and headed up the street. I weaved in and out of the small side streets—down Meadowbrook, along Cherokee, out Pioneer Trail, up West Ely—investigating all the nearby subdivisions. I blinked to hold back any more tears. I couldn't believe this nightmare was really happening.

My choice of subdivisions and my hopes were both nearly exhausted. I had just about given up any chance of ever seeing my papers again, when at the top of the hill, barely disappearing over the crest, I spied a garbage truck. There was no way of knowing if it was *my* garbage truck, but it was the first good lead I'd had. I jammed my foot on the accelerator and tore up the street.

When I crested the hill, there was no garbage truck in sight. The cadence of a marching army pounded in my ears. My mouth was so dry I couldn't swallow. Then, out of the corner of my eye, I glimpsed the truck heading onto a dead-end street.

On two tires, I turned the corner, intent on running down that garbage truck, when a second one came rolling up the street. My thoughts became a blur as I tried to decide what to do. "I'll catch the other truck on his way out," I mumbled. I screeched to a halt in the middle of the street, blocking all traffic, and leapt from my car, flagging my arms wildly at the approaching garbage truck.

A Don Johnson look-alike started to roll down his window. His sparkling blue eyes were filled with alarm. "Something wrong, lady? Do you need help?"

"Have you picked up any trash from Heritage Road this morning?" I demanded as I raced up to his truck.

"You mean that road off Surrey Hill?"

"Yes, yes." I ran my tongue nervously over my dry lips.

"Yeah, I was there. I have an appointment this afternoon, so I had to start earlier than usual—" Interrupting him, I began scaling the back of his garbage truck. Without asking permission, I vaulted both legs over and sank past my thighs into warm, sticky plastic trash bags. Flies delighted in this smorgasbord, buzzing from one entrée to the next. The aroma of overripe fruit and oily, metallic machinery hung in the air.

"My husband threw away some very important papers," I called down to the young man, now standing at the side of his truck. With his mouth agape, he stared, then shook his head.

"There's a full load of garbage up there, ma'am. As a matter of fact, I was just heading to the dump to unload."

Reality began to sink in slowly as I settled deeper into the mire of trash bags. I tried to wade through the swell of garbage, then stopped when a thought struck. All our neighbors had been considerate enough to use tidy plastic garbage bags, most of them cinched neatly with twist ties. I struggled through the piles, casting bags aside as I went, until I spotted a stained brown paper bag, partially hidden.

"There." I pointed. "I think I see my zucchini." I dived toward the front of the sludge pile. Heaving a plastic bag aside, I screamed, "Yes, that's my zucchini!"

I grabbed the zucchini off the top of the paper bag and tossed it aside. Underneath, rolled in a bundle, was the Sunday paper. Gently I swept off a sprinkling of coffee grounds and unfolded the newspaper. There, nestled in the middle of the entertainment section, lay my papers, totally unscathed by the surrounding filth. Tilting my head back, I shrieked with delight.

Momentarily I regained my senses, and I realized what a spectacle I must have presented to the poor young man still standing beside his truck.

Weak-kneed and aromatic, I made my way to the edge of the oversize garbage bin, where the young man politely helped me down. I apologized and thanked him repeatedly as he lined my car seat with clean newspapers. I drove slowly home, marveling at the chain of events. To have turned down the right street into the right subdivision, found the right truck, and then finally the right trash, seemed inconceivable.

I pulled into the driveway and noticed my husband's truck was gone. Our nosy neighbor sauntered over. "Your husband took off right after you. Said something about finding a garbage truck."

"Let him look," I said, laughing, feeling giddy and smug. "I found my papers." I held up the evidence. I still couldn't believe it.

Just as I entered the front door, my husband pulled up to the house. "I found my papers," I boasted.

"I know," he said, stepping out of his truck.

Feeling somewhat cheated out of my glory, I approached him. "How'd you know?" I asked, unable to contain my curiosity.

"I started to flag down a garbage truck, when the driver stuck his head out the window and yelled, 'Mister, she's already been here!'"

KARYN BUXMAN

WARRANTY X

One of the many challenges I was confronted with after my first husband's death was people calling and asking to speak to him. Paul was an attorney, and calls from clients and others unaware of his death continued for months.

One evening a couple of months after Paul's death, the phone rang. "Hello. Kleine-Kracht residence," I stated.

"May I speak to Paul Kleine-Kracht?" the caller said. I caught my breath and said, "I'm sorry, Paul is deceased. I'm his wife, may I help you?"

Without any comment about what I'd just said, the caller jumped right in with, "I'm John Jones with your appliance warranty center. I'm calling to remind you that the warranty on your appliance is about to expire and you need to renew it."

"Thank you for calling, but that appliance is several years old and I've decided not to renew the warranty."

With a tone of impatience, he responded, "Well, I'm sure your dead husband would want you to renew."

"Funny you should mention it, but just hours before Paul died, he said, 'Honey, whatever you do, don't renew the appliance warranty!'"

There was silence, and then Mr. Jones said, "Oh, okay," and hung up.

ANN E. WEEKS

THE PURPLE PEOPLE

My son Austin has always had a unique approach to life. He has been described as "imaginative," "full of life," and "quite the little character." Some of the more negative adjectives used to describe Austin are "hyper," "wild," and even "out of control." Having been his mother for all his six years of life, I have learned to take these comments in stride. I try to accept Austin just the way he is.

Lately, his favorite game is to pretend that his father and I are his "evil stepparents" and his "true parents" are the purple people from another planet who will one day rescue him. On a daily basis, I am still amused and amazed by the way this child views his world.

When he was five, Austin bounded down our flight of stairs and announced, "It's time to move on with my life." His plan was to pack all his "important things" and head out to face the "real world." Austin then turned on his heel and headed up the stairs to begin his new venture. I was not blessed with an immediate response, so I calmly made lunch. I then called Austin downstairs for some nutrition and a chat.

My approach was quick and to the point. I explained to Austin that by law, he was required to live with his dad and me until he was at least eighteen years old. Until then, we would try to make his time with us as happy and adventurous as possible. He thought about this for a while.

"Will Dad teach me to sword fight so I can fight off the bad guys?" he asked with concern. I assured him that his dad would be honored to.

"And will you teach me how to make pancakes, sausage, and eggs so I won't get hungry?" he asked.

"Sure, honey, I'd love to," I replied, stroking his hair. Austin solemnly nodded.

I was confident that we had struck an agreement and that Austin would be staying on with us for a while longer. He was silent as he finished his sandwich, and I cleared his plate away. Left sitting before him was a place mat with a map of the United States on it.

"Mom, where do we live?" Austin asked quietly.

Thankful for the change of subject, I pointed to the upper left corner of the map. "We live here, honey, in the state of Washington," I replied with enthusiasm.

"Oh. Well . . . in that case, I want to live here when I'm eighteen." Austin was pointing to the bottom right corner of the map, the tip of Florida, and the place farthest from us that he could imagine.

It is at times like these that I, too, wonder when the purple people will arrive!

JENNIFER HOWARD

*"I base most of my fashion taste
on what doesn't itch."*
—Gilda Radner

A CHRISTMAS SURPRISE INDEED!

When you live abroad, one of the most important things in life is getting mail from the family back home. The Christmas box from my son contained a red-and-white jogging suit.

The cheerful outfit was a pleasant change from my standard attire, blue jeans. I received several compliments the first time I wore my sporty new clothing to the office, amid a couple of guffaws about my new "Santa suit." I remained proud of my son's fine gift selection.

Imagine my shock when I received his next letter, in which he asked how I liked my new pajamas!

Roberta B. Jacobson

MORE CHOCOLATE STORIES?

Do you have a short story that fits the spirit of *Chocolate for a Woman's Heart* or *Chocolate for a Woman's Soul?* I am planning future editions using a similar format, which will feature love stories, inspirational stories, divine moments, and humorous events that teach us to laugh at ourselves. I seek heartwarming stories one to three pages in length that feed and lift the spirit, encourage us to go for our dreams, and tug at our emotions.

I invite you to join me in these future projects by sending your special story for consideration. If your story is selected, you will be listed as a contributing author, and you may include a biographical paragraph of your choice. For more information, or to send a story, please contact:

KAY ALLENBAUGH
P.O. Box 2165
Lake Oswego, OR 97035

CONTRIBUTORS

BURKY ACHILLES is a writer and recipient of a Walden Fellowship. She is working on her first novel, as well as a book of inspirational short stories. She and her husband are raising a daughter and a son on the brink of teenhood. (503) 638-4100.

ANN ALBERS is a traditional Reiki master, spiritual counselor, instructor, lecturer, and writer. She received her BS in Electrical Engineering from the University of Notre Dame and worked for eight years in the avionics industry before leaving to follow her spiritual calling. She is currently working on her first two books: *Whispers of the Spirit,* an inspiring and deeply human story of her spiritual awakening; and *No More Taboo!* to help women reclaim their bodies and their souls. (602) 485-1078.

BAILEY ALLARD is president of Allard Associates, Inc., an international seminar and consulting firm. She is a speaker, seminar leader, and business coach, who works with Fortune 500 companies on six continents. She speaks on influence and choicepoints in a downsized world. She is passionate about speaking to people—especially women—about understanding and acknowledging their value and increasing their influence. (919) 968-9900.

LORRI VAUGHTER ALLEN is a broadcast journalist and professional speaker. Her company, Good News!, helps people make more money and improve their image by mastering the media. (She's eaten a spudnut only once!) (972) 248-3610. <LorriA@wctv.com>

EMORY AUSTIN, Certified Speaking Professional, was featured in *Industry Week* magazine, along with fellow speakers Colin Powell, Margaret Thatcher, and Terry Anderson. She is a Phi Beta Kappa communications graduate of Wake Forest University and has keynoted in almost every industry, to rave reviews. For information regarding Emory's presentations and tapes, please call (704) 663-7575.

URSULA BACON fled Nazi Germany with her parents and spent the next nine years in China. She was interned, along with 18,000 European refugees, by Japanese occupation forces in Shanghai for four years. She emigrated to the United States at the end of WWII. Ursula is married to author Thorn Bacon, and they operate a small publishing house and write books. She is the coauthor of *Savage Shadows* (New York: New Horizon) and the author of *The Nervous Hostess Cookbook* (BookPartners, 1998). (503) 682-9821.

JENNIFER BROWN BANKS is a Chicago-based writer, poet, and speaker. She has been a contributing writer for *Being Single* magazine since 1995, providing insightful perspectives on love, relationships, self-esteem, and divine principles. She is founder of Poets United to Advance the Arts, and author of three collections of poetry: *Meet Me in the Middle, Amidst Quiet Hours,* and *Under the Influence of Love*. She credits her mother, Arabella, for motivation and her son, Jaremy, for inspiration. (773) 509-8018.

T. J. BANKS of Avon, Connecticut, has written fiction, poetry, book reviews, and essays for numerous publications, including *Poets and Writers, Cat Fancy, Just Cats!, Writing for Our Lives, Woman & Earth,* and *Our Mothers Our Selves: Writers and Poets Celebrate Motherhood*. She is an editorial associate with the Writer's Digest School and has won awards for her fiction and journalism from the Cat Writers' Association and *The Writing Self*. She has written a novel for young adults, *Houdini*. (860) 678-7978.

CAROLE BELLACERA is a writer living in Manassas, Virginia. Her fiction and articles have appeared in over 200 magazines in America and abroad. She recently optioned her first screenplay, *Border Crossings*, to Rialto Films for development as a cable-TV movie. In the years since she met Frank and became the mother of Leah, twenty-one, and Stephen, eighteen, she has worked as a medical technician, a sales clerk, a typist, a library aide, a secretary, and a receptionist for a congressman on Capitol Hill. But she is still proudest to be Frank's wife. <KaroBella@aol.com>

ANN BENSON is the author of the novel *The Plague Tales* and four best-sellers on beadwork. She is currently working on another novel.

DEBRA AYERS BROWN is the mother of an energetic second-grade student and is the senior vice president of Printgraphix. She has won numerous national design and writing awards. The author of several inspirational and children's stories, she is currently working on a mystery novel series. She is the mayor's wife and "First Lady of Hinesville, Georgia." (800) 257-9734.

ARLINE CRAWFORD BURTON is now a patient representative in a hospital in Georgia. She is a lover of mankind—God's greatest creation. Kindness, love, and understanding are her tools. The smiles her story "Angel of the Lord" brings are her reward.

KARYN BUXMAN, RN, MS, is from Hannibal, Missouri—home of the other great humorist, Mark Twain. She was editor for the American Association for Therapeutic Humor and is vice president of *Journal of Nursing Jocularity,* a national humor magazine for nurses. A leading national expert on therapeutic humor, Karyn Buxman wows audiences across the country with programs like "Is the Noise in My Head Bothering You?" and "JEST for Success." She has written countless articles and produced numerous audio and video tapes. To see how your group can benefit from some "mirth aid," contact Karyn at 1-800-8HUMORX. <www.humorx.com>

MARY CARROLL-HACKETT is a writer, a student, but first and foremost a mom, who lives with her family in eastern North

Carolina. When she's not chasing the three Irish-fairy children who inhabit her home, she is at work on her first novel.

MICHELLE COHEN is a former social worker with the developmentally disabled and a longtime public speaker and volunteer to the AIDS community. She has written a thriller and is currently working on a nonfiction collaborative work with her mother, Eileen Davis, titled *Dear Mush (Letters Between a Mother and Daughter)*. (973) 597-9212.

CONSTANCE CONACE worked full time and raised two sons as a single mother and has now returned to college to pursue a degree in English. Her goal is to write and enjoy life and her family to the fullest.

CARMEN D'AMICO resides in Fort Lauderdale, Florida, and is an international speaker, actress, author, and celebrity look-alike for Elizabeth Taylor. She has appeared on radio and television and has helped raise money for AIDS through numerous benefits and appearances. Her life experiences of triumphs over tragedies have made her a survivor. Her focus on restoring self-esteem has inspired her audiences. Her book, *Dust in the Wind*, is for anyone searching for hope, enlightenment, and strength. (954) 772-4111.

RITA DAVENPORT is president of Arbonne International, a personal care product company. She is a charter member of the National Speakers Association and has been awarded the Certified Speaking Professional (CSP) designation. She was honored by NSA with their highest lifetime award: the Council of Peers Award for Excellence (CPAE). She is a nationally known success-seminar leader, keynote speaker, humorist, and best-selling author of several books, including *Making Time, Making Money*. She produced and hosted her award-winning TV show for fifteen years in Phoenix. Her cable TV show, *Success Strategies*, was viewed in over 32 million homes. She has also appeared on

ABC's *Good Morning America* and other national shows. (602) 482-6919.

EILEEN DAVIS is a writer of poetry, short stories, and novels. She is working on a collaborative nonfiction work with her daughter, Michelle Cohen entitled *Dear Mush (Letters Between a Mother and Daughter)*. She has completed a collection of reflective short stories entitled *Of Me I Sing*, and a novel, *Yesterday I Woke Up Dead*.

LINDA DUNIVIN, MEd, has won several awards for lyrics in songwriting. She performed on the video of her collaborative children's musical, *Together*, which was published for Christian television. An inspirational and juvenile writer, she is currently writing a romantic historical novel. She is a former teacher of the visually impaired, has a Master of Education degree from Georgia State University, and lives on Colonel's Island, south of Savannah.

ANAMAE ELLEDGE is an elementary school teacher in the Hawaii public school system. In her spare time, she enjoys reading, quilting, and taking care of her six children.

LINDA G. ENGEL earned her master's degree in communication disorders and was a speech-language clinician and coordinator in public schools for twenty years prior to the adoption of a son and daughter. As a freelancer, she writes short stories for regional publications and is currently working on a book about grief. She resides with her husband and children in the heart of the Minnesota lakes, where she was born and raised. (218) 829-3433.

HOLLY ESPARZA, RN, MBA, has been a registered nurse, manager, and sometimes even a leader for many years. She is currently the director for Women's and Children's Services for two hospitals in Denver, Colorado. Her passion is health and wellness, and encouraging herself, her husband, and their two daughters to live a healthy, happy, balanced life. (303) 741-5203.

CANDIS FANCHER, MS, CCC in Speech Pathology, is the founder of Inner Sources. Audiences are inspired by her upbeat philosophy. Her Pleasure Pause seminars have energized participants to adopt more positive lifestyles. Her Staying Afloat in the Stresspools of Life seminars explore practical ideas for integrating humor into your personal and professional life. Her SNAC approach provides practical and humorous ways for Stopping, Noticing, Acting, and Creating heart-to-heart connections. She is also a speech/voice coach and is a member of the American Speech-Language Hearing Association and the National Speakers Association. (612) 890-3897.

JILL FANCHER, born in Seoul, Korea, attends school at Nicollet Junior High in Burnsville, Minnesota. She loves soccer, piano, oboe, and her dog, Ashley. Chad, her older brother, is her hero. She is enthusiastic, has a great sense of humor, and enjoys being with her friends. She is the daughter of Candis Fancher.

HOLLY FITZHARDINGE is a writer and film director in Vancouver, B.C., and has worked extensively in story development and production in both films and television. She is a member of the Directors Guild and Writers Guild and recently completed a film concerning Amnesty International prisoners of conscience, which is on the film festival circuit. She is currently working on another film. Fax: (604) 940-8814.

JOEANN FOSSLAND, President of Advantage Solutions Group, is a personal and business coach and professional speaker who lives in the beautiful Sonoran Desert of Tucson, Arizona. She delights in working with individuals, groups, and companies that are committed to discovering how to maximize their uniqueness. Through keynotes, workshops, and one-on-one coaching, Joeann's clients create abundance, love, and creativity that ignite joy, self-expression, and aliveness! (520) 744-8731. <Joeann@aol.com>

JUDITH MORTON FRASER, MA, is also a Marriage/Family/Child Therapist and an actress. Her published works include the stories "Alone in the Woods Bearly" (*L.A. Times* and L.A. Times Syndicate) and "Grammas Don't Die" (Everywomans Village); a poem, "To Know You" (Hallmark); and articles dealing with relationships and addictions (California Association of Marriage & Family Therapists newsletters). She is presently writing a novel combining creativity, Native American ceremonies, and life passages. Her musical director husband, Ian, is an eleven Emmy Award winner; daughter Tiffany is an actress; son Neal is a chef; grandchildren Grace, Chelsea, and Jenna are creative works in progress. (213) 656-9800.

MARCI MADSEN FULLER is a writer, wife, and mother, currently living in south Texas, with the wild parrots, and water snakes and the geckos that bob their heads in greeting from the kitchen windowsill. She has just finished her first novel and is now sorting inspirations for her second. (956) 399-3094. <Wlflsprite@aol.com>

JILL GOODWIN considers herself to be a student of spirituality on a guided journey by her Higher Power. She is a published reporter and interviewer, and has hosted a television series. She has a BS in communications and works as a public relations practitioner in media relations. (713) 212-0486.

MAUREEN GORSUCH is a Licensed Massage Therapist who is presently living and working in Kansas City, Missouri. She grew up in New York, then moved to Kailua Kona, Hawaii, where she continued her education and enjoyed great friends and sunsets. She loves skydiving, exercise, and meditation, and can sometimes be found writing in her journal while sipping wine in an ethnic restaurant. (816) 765-6297.

CINDY HANSON is an air personality at KINK-FM in Portland, Oregon. She is a seeker of cosmic truth, a believer in the healing powers of nature, the great outdoors, art, and music. She has an unbridled passion for the Oregon coast and other unspoiled wide-open spaces. She is an artist in the media of stained glass and watercolors, an aspiring poet and essayist, a singer of silly songs, avid cyclist and runner, and an occasional hospice volunteer. (503) 226-5100 x6224.

DONNA HARTLEY is an international speaker, a change specialist, and a member of the National Speakers Association. Owner and founder of Hartley International, she has been featured on NBC, ABC, PBS, The Learning Channel, and in the *New York Times*. Her popular book, video, and audio training series is called "Get What You Want." (800) 438-9428.

CHRISTINE HARVEY is a TV and radio personality and the author of five books in twenty languages, including *Secrets of the World's Top Sales Performers*, which has sold 150,000 copies. She is a keynote conference speaker, who addresses audiences small and large, including Sony, IBM, Toyota, Lloyds Bank, Mortgage Brokers Associations, Century 21, and writers conferences. She's an active director of the board of an investment bank and a venture capital company, and is a council member of the International Center of the National Speakers Association. She divides her time between her office in London, her home in Brussels, and her work in the U.S., including television programs in Los Angeles. (800) 813-7197.

MARIE HEGEMAN, CSW, holds a BS in psychology from the State University of New York at Oneonta and a master's degree in social work from SUNY-Albany. She is a clinical social worker (psychotherapist) who practices in Oneonta, New York. She is writing a book about her mother's extraordinary battle against cancer. (607) 432-7285.

Contributors

LIZ CURTIS HIGGS is a Certified Speaking Professional and has earned the Council of Peers Award for Excellence with the National Speakers Association. She writes a bimonthly column for *Today's Christian Woman*, called "Life with Liz," and is a member of the American Association for Therapeutic Humor, the Fellowship of Merry Christians, and the National Association for Professionals in Women's Health. She is the author of four humorous books for women: *One Size Fits All and Other Fables; Only Angels Can Wing It, the Rest of Us Have to Practice; Mirror, Mirror on the Wall, Have I Got News for You!;* and *Forty Reasons Why Life Is More Fun After the Big 4-0.* Her four children's books include: *The Pumpkin Patch Parable; The Parable of the Lily; The Sunflower Parable;* and *The Pine Tree Parable.* (800) 762-6565.

ELLEN URBANI HILTEBRAND, MA, is an author and art therapist practicing in Portland, Oregon, where she specializes in developing art therapy programs to meet the psychosocial needs of physically ill patients and their families. Her company, Healing Arts, provides national contracting and consulting services to health care organizations interested in developing therapeutic arts programs, and she speaks regularly at medical conferences throughout the country. The therapeutic school art program she developed while serving as a Peace Corps Volunteer in Guatemala is now used worldwide by Peace Corps Volunteers and other development workers. A book about her experiences there should be completed within the next year. (503) 413-8404. <hiltebrand@juno.com>

JENNIFER HOWARD lives in White Salmon, Washington, with her husband and their four sons. She enjoys gardening, horseback riding, and spending time with her family and friends. Writing is a hobby that she uses to capture the milestones in her children's lives. (509) 493-4701.

SHEILA S. HUDSON, founder of Bright Ideas, is a freelance writer and speaker living in Athens, Georgia. An award-winning writer, she enjoys credits in magazines such as *Christian Stan-*

dard, *Lookout, Reminisce, Athens, Teddy Bear, Just Between Us,* and *The Pastor's Family.* She and Tim have been married twenty-nine years and have two grown daughters and a grandson; they begin their sixteenth year at the Christian Campus Fellowship at the University of Georgia. (706) 546-5085 voice/fax. <sheila@naccm.org>

ANTIONETTE VIGLIATURO ISHMAEL is the fifth–sixth grade language arts teacher at St. Bernadette Catholic School in Kansas City, Missouri. She was a 1997 recipient of the Excellence in Teaching Award in Missouri. She is also a writer, scout leader, the wife of Phil, and—most of all—the proud mother of Patrick (fourteen), Anthony (eleven), and Dominic (eight). (816) 231-4138.

ROBERTA B. JACOBSON, PhD, has lived in Europe for over twenty years. Her freelance writing reflects (mostly Western) European themes and has been published in *Transitions Abroad, True Experience, Cats, McCall's, Writer's Digest,* and *The American.* Her poems have appeared in *The Christian Science Monitor, Wry Bred!, Cicada, Krax,* and *Haiku.* <100601.3415@compuserve.com>

DEBB JANES is a radio news director and morning radio personality in Portland, Oregon. She successfully helped lobby for changes in Oregon's stalking laws when she encountered legal problems trying to prevent a stalker from harassing her. She is currently co-creating a talk show that features positive role models and programs for and about women. She's the mother of three terrific children. They are joined by an old soul cat and a wonder dog. (503) 226-9791.

SARAH JORDAN is a mother, wife, writer, and advocate for home education. As co-owner of Mindfull, she organizes ReThinking Education conferences and mothers' retreats and lectures on all types of family matters. She lives in the small town of Double Oak, Texas, just north of the Dallas–Fort Worth Metroplex, with her three home-schooled children and longtime friend, editor, and husband, Gary. (817) 430-4835.

LISA JUSCIK is the assistant director of athletic media services at Northwestern University in Evanston, Illinois (847) 733-8074.

KATHI J. KEMPER, MD, MPH, is an internationally known pediatrician, educator, author, and researcher. She is the author of the widely acclaimed book *The Holistic Pediatrician* and president-elect of the Ambulatory Pediatric Association. Her greatest life adventure and joy is being Daniel's mom.

NANCY KIERNAN, PhD, is an educator, a professional speaker, and a cancer survivor. She is committed to helping raise awareness for others with life-threatening problems by writing and speaking about the proved links between chronobiology and one's medical choices. Her current book in progress reveals many little-known truths about "perfect timing" and helps a woman plan strategically for a healthy life. (602) 391-9132. <AZKiernan@AOL.com>

SHARON KINDER is currently writing about her numerous spiritual experiences. Having successfully made the transformation from business owner and community leader to writer and hermit, she has recently moved to the Pacific Northwest from her home in the Sierra Nevada foothills of Central California. (503) 543-8262.

MARLENE L. KING, MA, is a professional writer, artist, and dreamologist. She currently publishes an interactive dream column in Dream Network and is writing a book exploring creation theories and symbology. She consults and does contract work for individuals, groups, and businesses. (541) 471-9337. <marlene@chatlink.com>

TAMMY KLING is a freelance writer, speaker, and the author of *Searching for a Piece of My Soul—How to Find a Missing Family*

Member or Loved One. She specializes in talks on adoption, family searches and reunions, and crisis management. She spent years serving on an emergency response team for a global airline and is currently working on her first novel, *Impact.* (972) 248-1429.

LON MY LAM is a teacher in Honolulu. She was born in Vietnam but raised in Oregon and California before settling in Hawaii. Her greatest ambition is to live each day fully with integrity, patience, and love. (808) 623-7897.

SUSAN LAMAIRE has spent the four years since college graduation trying various methods of rent payment (waitress, substitute teacher, bookseller). She relies on her quick wit, ingenuity, and God's power to get her from one trial to the next. She has a reputation for putting her foot in her mouth and rebelling against authority. She has a degree from Bucknell University and is a freelance writer currently working as a substitute teacher. (732) 477-6083.

CATHERINE LANIGAN has been writing for seventeen years and is the author of fifteen novels, including the novelizations of *Romancing the Stone* and *Jewel of the Nile.* She introduced a new breed of heroine into the literary fold, "The Evolving Woman," a woman who builds an arsenal of wisdom, dignity, and courage that will fortify her capacity to love and be loved despite her battles with very real tragedies and crises. Her self-empowerment stems from an abiding spiritual faith, which guides her and continually renews hope. (212) 929-1222.

STEPHANIE LAURIDSEN has been a news producer for Westcott Communications in Carrollton, Texas, since November 1992. She produces, reports, writes, shoots, and edits for the Automotive Satellite Television Network. As co-coordinator for the Westcott Communications Internship program, she frequently speaks at Texas universities to recruit new interns. As an automotive journalist, she also serves as the first female president of the Texas Automotive Writers Association. She is active in her

Christian life as a Senior High Youth Group Counselor and accompanies the group twice a year to continue the youth mission in Acuna, Mexico. (941) 540-9911.

MARY LOVERDE, MS, ANP, is a professional speaker and founder of Life Balance, Inc. Her passion is researching new ways to balance career success with a happy and healthy family. She is the author of *Stop Screaming at the Microwave: How to Connect Your Disconnected Life* (New York: Fireside/Simon & Schuster 1998) and has produced an audiotape series entitled *June Cleaver Never Fried Bacon in a Bill Blass Dress*. For information about her customized Memory Jar and Memory Cards, please call (303) 755-5806.

JILL LYNNE, a photographer and writer, is known internationally for her special portraits of VIPs, documentation of popular culture, environmental nature studies, use of cutting-edge technology and alternative photographic techniques. With twenty-one solo exhibitions, her photography is represented in prestigious collections, and her photography and writing have appeared in *Newsweek, Vogue Italia, Ms.,* and The *Miami Herald*. Based in New York City and Miami, she also produces special promotional and fund-raising events for such organizations as the United Nations, the Nature Conservancy, and the American Foundation for AIDS Research. (212) 741-2409 or (305) 532-8096.

CHRISTINE D. MAREK is a thirty-three-year-old mother and wife, who presently works as an industrial electrician. Christine began writing for therapeutic reasons while in counseling to end a violent marriage and to heal from her own childhood sexual abuse. Much to her surprise, as Christine began to heal, she began to connect with a gift that had heretofore remained under wraps. (815) 258-7788.

LYNNE MASSIE is a business consultant, speaker, and coach, who mobilizes people by training them in both personal and professional development. She is also a cancer survivor, who has written a book about her intense and inspiring journey through cancer, called *The Buttercup Has My Smile*. (503) 675-0058.

SUSAN MILES is a writer and photographer. Her current series, "The Heart of the Flower," depicts the inner beauty of nature through macrophotography. Her images are available as prints and on greeting cards. (503) 282-6266.

MARY MANIN MORRISSEY holds a master's degree in Psychology. Her growing global audience is a tribute to her inspirational speaking and teaching ministry. She counsels and leads seminars reaching thousands each year as the founder and spiritual leader of the Living Enrichment Center, often referred to as a model of the 21st Century Church. She is the author of *Building Your Field of Dreams*. (503) 682-5683.

YOLANDA NAVA is a television broadcaster, writer, and consultant. She is host of *Life and Times*, a nightly newscast that airs on KCET/TV in Los Angeles, and she writes a weekly column for Eastern Group Publications, the largest chain of bilingual newspapers in the nation. She is currently writing her first book, *It's All in the Frijoles: A Book of Hispanic Virtues*, to be published by Fireside/Simon & Schuster in 1999. (213) 256-7836.

O. C. O'CONNELL is a freelance writer who still struggles with her hair from time to time. She resides with her beloved and their twin angel babies in a perpetual state of chaos, passion, and negotiation, which are elemental in a house of four fiercely loving interdependent souls. She has led past lives as a teacher of English, algebra, and geometry, a market research analyst, and a vice president of corporate communications. She has never been a hairstylist. (303) 730-6745.

DEBORAH OLIVE, senior minister at Unity Center of Tacoma, in Tacoma, Washington, skillfully navigated the corporate world as a sales representative in the medical field prior to attending ministerial school. She holds a bachelor's degree in biochemistry and artfully bridges the arenas of spirituality, science, and business. Deborah's ministry, characterized by her integrity, humor, and commitment to spiritual transformation, supports people in clearing the obstacles to their heart's desires and achieving their dreams. (253) 460-9898. <Soulnheart@aol.com>

MARY OMWAKE has been the senior minister of Unity Church of Overland Park in Kansas since 1989. Under her leadership, the congregation has grown from under 200 to 2,450 members. She is a founding member of the Association for Global New Thought and is committed to supporting authentic spiritual growth and rendering genuine service to an awakening world. (913) 649-1750.

CHASSIDY A. F. PERSONS holds a BA in Latin American and Caribbean Studies. She is a preschool teacher working on her master's in Special Education. (518) 887-5898.

CINDY POTTER is the executive director of the Oregon State Mortuary and Cemetery Board, which is responsible for the professional licensing and regulation of the death care industry. She and her husband, Dan, reside in Beaverton, Oregon, and share their lives with three cats and three dogs. During their twenty-four-year marriage, they have rescued and either found the homes of or found new homes for over two hundred stray animals. Dazy Joy was their first. (503) 524-3614.

DIANE RIPSTEIN, MEd, is a speaker and trainer and the principal of Diane Ripstein Consulting in Newton, Massachusetts. She helps her clients give more powerful presentations, more succinct sales pitches, more compelling investment-raising road shows, and more credible interviews to the media. With both a highly successful sales career and several years of onstage performance experience behind her, Diane specializes in high energy. (617) 630-8630.

ROBIN RYAN is an international pilot for United Airlines, a wife and mother. She delights in giving inspirational speeches and motivating people of all ages to "go for the gold" and follow their dreams, no matter how seemingly difficult. She has begun an inspirational book using her life experiences as a basis for her message that if she can reach her goal, anyone can dig deep inside herself, dare to dream, and accomplish her dearest desires. (360) 576-5600.

JOANNA SLAN is a professional speaker and the author of *I'm Too Blessed to Be Depressed* and *Using Stories and Humor: Grab Your Audience*. Audiences around the world have enjoyed her uplifting and insightful stories on the topics of teamwork, change, communications, conflict, and workplace productivity. She still rocks Michael in their home in St. Louis, but now that's he's a big guy of eight, it's a lot harder to get all of him onto her lap. For more information about Joanna's speaking services or to order her books, call 1-888-BLESSED (253-7733). <JoannaSlan@aol.com>

JODY STEVENSON, director of Soul Purpose Ministries, teaches comprehensive technology that accelerates soulful awareness toward the discovery of your special contribution to humanity, your soul's purpose. Her delight is assisting you to awaken to your personal passions. Author of *Soul Purpose*, and *Solutions*, she is currently a counselor in private practice, speaking nationally and leading seminars on creative expression and Soul Purpose Principles. (503) 977-2235.

LINDA ROSS SWANSON is a freelance writer who frequently publishes essays and poetry. She is currently completing her first book, *Beheading the Hydrangea*. (503) 292-4755.

KATE MCKERN VERIGIN is a licensed minister who focuses her energies on creating ritual and ceremony to celebrate all aspects of life. She is in her fourth year of leading moon ceremonies for women. On Friday nights, Kate serves as minister to a group called Heart & Soul, which sponsors eclectic ceremonies for women, men, and children designed to open the heart and celebrate the soul. By degree she is an educator and communicator. Through life experience she is an Emmy Award–winning television producer, publicist, spiritual counselor, and mentor, wife, stepmom, and cat lover. She lives in Portland, Oregon. (503) 256-9833.

ANN E. WEEKS, DNS, RN, is a nationally known speaker and nurse family therapist who gives her audiences and clients many everyday strategies to heal the stresses of life's passages. Her ever-present sense of humor and real-life stories always make her presentations a treat. She is the author of seven books and owns Passages Publishing, a small press dedicated to putting into print the stories that pass on our experience and heritage. She is a self-described "recovering academic" and is former dean and associate professor of the Lansing School of Nursing, Education and Health Sciences. She is a consultant on organizational communication and team building and innovative programs, and has twenty years' experience as a legal expert witness. (502) 458-2461. <healingpassages@ka.net>

ALICE STERN WEISER, a native Bostonian, is a graduate of Boston University. She received her certification from the International Society of Graphoanalysis. A leading expert in handwriting analysis, body language, and voice inflection, she was elected the 1995 International Handwriting Analyst. She is a popular motivational speaker, teacher, TV guest, workshop headliner, jury analyst, and personnel consultant. Her lectures not only entertain and inform but promote confidence through nonverbal communication skills. (713) 270-1645.

JEAN WENZEL has lived in Sierra Leone, Iceland, Germany, the Faeroe Islands, and Pakistan before settling in what she believes to be the most beautiful place of all, Oregon. She writes for magazines, newspapers, and web sites, teaches writing, and hosts and anchors on community radio. She is an all-weather hiker, a voracious reader, and a master knitter.

ACKNOWLEDGMENTS

My deepest gratitude goes to the contributors of this book. Their unique and contagious enthusiasm and their willingness to share their favorite "heart" stories created the magic and universal appeal of *Chocolate for a Woman's Heart*.

Many thanks and the warmest regards to my agent, Peter Miller, who opens doors and makes things happen, and my editor, Becky Cabaza, for her expertise, friendship, and belief in me.

A special thanks to: Ellen Hiltebrand, a gifted writer and friend, for reworking several stories; motivational speakers Mary LoVerde, Candis Fancher, Donna Hartley, Emory Austin, Irene Levitt. April Kemp, Maggie Bedrosian, and Joanna Slan for their special love of the *Chocolate* series and their understanding of its value to readers. My love and appreciation go to my publicist extraordinaire Joanne McCall, and to Kathie Millett, Linda Kemp, Jody Stevenson, Susan Miles, Linda Swanson, Michelle Hayhurst, Ursula Bacon, Mary Jo Evans, and Jacqui Elliott for their support, feedback, and friendship.

As always, my heartfelt love and appreciation to my one-in-a-million husband, Eric, whose integrity and commitment in his professional and personal life is beyond reproach. He makes our journey together a playful adventure.

Thanks to my family for their understanding and patience during the "creative process"—and to my daddy, to whom this book is dedicated.

The sweet, delicious bonus from compiling these stories has been the new friendships of seventy-four women from around the country. I am grateful for their generosity, and I'm honored to have their stories in *Chocolate for a Woman's Heart*.

PERMISSIONS ACKNOWLEDGMENTS

"The Minister and Me" is an excerpt from *Only the Angels Can Wing It, The Rest of Us Have to Practice,* by permission of Thomas Nelson Publishers, Nashville, Tennessee, © 1995 by Liz Curtis Higgs.

"United States of Motherhood" is an excerpt from *I'm Too Blessed to Be Depressed: Stories to Move You from Stressed to Blessed,* with permission of Joanna Slan, © 1997 by Joanna Slan.

"Healing with Love" is an edited excerpt from *Building Your Field of Dreams,* by permission of Bantam Books, a division of Bantam Doubleday Dell Publishing Group, Inc., New York, New York, © 1996 by Mary Manin Morrissey.

ABOUT THE AUTHOR

Kay Allenbaugh is the author of *Chocolate for a Woman's Soul* and *Chocolate for a Woman's Heart*. She resides with her husband, Eric, in Lake Oswego, Oregon.

DON'T MISS THE FIRST VOLUME OF DELICIOUS CHOCOLATE STORIES!

Chocolate for a Woman's Soul

77 Stories to Feed Your Spirit and Warm Your Heart

KAY ALLENBAUGH

"This book will feed your soul and fuel your dreams. You'll believe that anything is possible."

—Debbi Fields, Entrepreneur and author of *Mrs. Fields' I Love Chocolate! Cookbook*

____	Chocolate for a Woman's Soul	0-684-83217-8	$11.00
____	Chocolate for a Woman's Soul Audiobook	0-671-57964-9	$16.00
____	Chocolate for a Woman's Heart	0-684-84896-1	$11.00
____	Chocolate for a Woman's Heart Audiobook	0-671-58223-2	$16.00

Simon & Schuster, Inc. Date:_____
200 Old Tappan Road, Old Tappan, NJ 07675. Mail Order Dept.
Please send me copies of the above titles.

☐ Save! Enclose full amount per copy with this coupon. Publisher pays postage and handling; or charge my credit card. ☐ MasterCard ☐ Visa

My credit card number is _____ Card expires _____
Signature _____
Name _____
Address _____
City _____ State _____ Zip _____
Or available at your local bookstore.   Prices subject to change without notice.